TEACHERS' GUIDE TO THE COMMODORE COMPUTER

TEACHERS' GUIDE TO THE COMMODORE COMPUTER

BASIC Programming and Classroom Applications

SUSAN ELSHAW THRALL
FRED A. SPRINGER

SAGE PUBLICATIONS
Beverly Hills   London   New Delhi

For information address:

SAGE Publications, Inc.
275 South Beverly Drive
Beverly Hills, California 90212

SAGE Publications India Pvt. Ltd.   SAGE Publications Ltd
C-236 Defence Colony   28 Banner Street
New Delhi 110 024, India   London EC1Y 8QE, England

Printed in the United States of America

Library of Congress Cataloging in Publication Data

Thrall, Susan Elshaw.
   Teachers' guide to the Commodore computer.

   Bibliography: p.
   1. Education—Computer programs. 2. Education—
Data processing. 3. BASIC (Computer program language).
I. Springer, Fred A. II. Title.
LB1028.43.T47   1984   371.3′9445   84-4737
ISBN 0-8039-2311-2 (pbk.)

FIRST PRINTING

CONTENTS

PREFACE

Because microcomputers are fast becoming a part of almost every school system, many teachers are attempting to familiarize themselves with the use of the new computer technology for the classroom. This book was written in response to teachers who requested a basic handbook to guide them in three areas: (1) the operation of the microcomputer, (2) learning the programming language BASIC, and (3) the effective use of the microcomputer in the classroom.

This book is deliberately terse. It is aimed at those who must quickly grasp the new technology and use this tool efficiently and effectively. This book may be read on its own, or as part of courses on computer programming or educational applications of the microcomputer. This book is intended to guide the teacher quickly and thoroughly through the fundamentals of using the microcomputer. It is the teachers who must put the microcomputers to work in their classroom now.

This book will teach teachers (1) how to operate the microcomputer (Chapters 2 and 6); (2) the BASIC programming language (Chapter 3 and Appendix A); and (3) educational applications of the microcomputer in the classroom (Chapters 4, 5, and 6).

Chapter 2 outlines the basic operation of the Commodore computer, cursor control, using the computer as a calculator, loading and saving a program from a cassette and disk, and the operation of a printer. The fourth part of Chapter 6 also presents a short guide to operating the Commodore computer.

Important BASIC programming statements are presented in Chapter 3 in the form of short discussions, sample programs and related questions, and exercises. The answers to all questions and exercises are located in Appendix A.

Chapter 4 on educational applications is divided into 4 subsections. The first subsection discusses the utility of using a microcomputer as a teaching aid. In the second subsection, a chart describes the various uses of the computer in the classroom including the interactive role between computer, student, and teacher. The third subsection describes the administrative uses of the microcomputer. The final subsection contains a guide to the schedule and use of microcomputers if the computer-to-student ratio is small.

Chapter 5 and 6 also contain educational applications of the microcomputer. In Chapter 5, several programs for enjoyment and reinforcement of previously learned skills are listed; these include a clock program, a music program, a drawing program, and an animation program. Chapter 6 helps the educator in (1) the selection of good software; (2) helping users recover from computer or software failure; and (3) easing other teachers into the use of microcomputers in the classroom.

This book also provides supplemental material in Chapter 1 and Appendixes B and C that will be of interest to most teachers. Topics include a brief history of the computer, an explanation of the principal components of the computer, a glossary of frequently used microcomputer terminology, and a resource list of books and periodicals related to the educational use of the microcomputer.

Charts and reference guide instructions are included that can be posted at the computer center or throughout the classroom or used for personal reference. These include instructions on how to recover from computer or software failure, a summary page of operating instructions, a list of limits and peculiarities of the Commodore (PET), a guide to the optimal use of the microcomputer, advice on what to look for when buying good software, and ways to foster positive attitudes on the part of less-than enthusiastic fellow teachers.

Because our book is a handbook, with the exception of Chapter 3 on BASIC programming, any sections and subsections can be read independently of the others without losing continuity of thought.

However, in the BASIC programming chapter, we recommend reading the sections in the order that they appear since each succeeding section builds upon the previous section. Sample programs and exercises assume knowledge of the BASIC statements contained in the preceding sections; those previously learned statements are continually practiced so they become a part of the teacher's active computer vocabulary.

Teachers are aware that the most effective method of learning is to have the students actually doing something, not just reading or listening. We apply this principle especially in the BASIC programming language sections where the user is encouraged to run the Sample Programs and observe the results.

The suggested procedure for these BASIC programming sections is as follows:

(1) Read the short introduction to each section carefully.
(2) Type the Sample Programs *exactly* as shown into the microcomputer and run them, observing the results.
(3) Answer the questions following the Sample Programs and check the answers in Appendix A if necessary.
(4) Write the programs in the Exercises to synthesize knowledge and also to get a bank of programs useful in the classroom.
(5) Use each section as is or modify it as necessary in your own lesson plans on the microcomputer.

This book is mainly for users of Commodore microcomputers: the PET, CBM, Commodore 64, and the Vic 20.[1] These microcomputers are similar in operation; the differences between them are generally limited to sound generation, use of color, and various keyboard options.

We keep our discussion limited to that which is common to the Commodore computers. Although our general focus is the PET, we have deliberately avoided features peculiar to one or two of them and not to the other(s).

All BASIC programs in this book have been tested on the PET 4032. They will work equally as well on the C64 and Vic 20. Any minor modifications to be made are noted in the text.

With this information, you should be ready to jump into computing. Good luck in your microcomputing ventures!

Our thanks go to Grant Thrall, Department of Geography, University of Florida, for his constructive suggestions and encouragement.

—Susan Elshaw Thrall
Fred A. Springer

NOTE

1. PET, CBM, Commodore 64, and Vic 20 are registered trademarks of Commodore Business Machines, Inc., a division of Commodore International. Other registered trademarks include the following: Acorn—Acorn Computers Corp.; Apple—Apple Computers Inc.; Atari—Atari, Inc.; Max-80—LOBO Systems, Inc.; Sinclair—Sinclair Research Ltd.; Timex—Timex Computer Corp.; TRS-80—Radio Shack Division of Tandy Corp.

1 Introduction

- History of the Computer
- The Major Parts of the Computer

HISTORY OF THE COMPUTER

Man's use of calculating aids predates recorded history. A pile of twigs, counting stones, marks on paper, huge monoliths like Stonehenge, and small hand-held devices such as the abacus have all helped people to manipulate numbers and data.

Modern electronic computers have a relatively short history. Charles Babbage (1791-1871), an English mathematician, is considered the inventor of the first computer. Called the Difference Engine, it was a large assembly of wheels, levers, cogs, and gears. Babbage envisioned his machine being able to solve polynomial equations and even print out the answers. The mechanics did not inspire nineteenth century government or business to provide the necessary capital; hence Babbage's calculating engine never was made operational.

About the same time a French inventor Joseph Jacquard was using a card with punched holes to control the patterns on a weaving loom. This was one of the first times an input device—a punched card—was used to "program" a machine.

During World War II and the ensuing two decades, the development of the electronic computer really "took off." Computers now used electrical impulses instead of mechanical gears. These computers were initially developed for interpreting spy codes, handling large amounts of information about the enemy and aiding plane and submarine warfare. Machines of this generation required a large amount of power; they required special air conditioned rooms because they used vacuum tubes which generate large amounts of heat. For example, the ENIAC (Electronic Numerical Integrator and Calculator) built in 1946 by the United States military needed a special cooling system because it used 140 kilowatts of power.

With the invention of transistors the vacuum tubes were quickly replaced. The transistors were smaller, faster, more reliable, and they did not heat up like the vacuum tubes. The computer could now be moved out of its strictly controlled cool environment and into an ordinary office or laboratory.

In 1959, the first integrated circuit or "chip" was developed. A chip is composed of a piece of silicon upon which circuits are photographically imprinted. Just as transistors replaced the vacuum tube, chips replaced standard transistors in computers.

Since 1959, chips have become smaller; in others words, the same size chip has had an increase in the amount of circuits it could hold. With this simultaneous decrease in size/increase in memory power, the size and price of computers has dramatically decreased. The sales of computers to industry and businesses, and now recently to schools and homes, have risen at an increasing rate. Computers are becoming a ubiquitous part of our environment.

THE MAJOR PARTS OF THE COMPUTER

CENTRAL PROCESSING UNIT

— the intelligence of the computer
— is the microprocessor chip in the microcomputer
— made up of control unit and arithmetic unit

Control Unit

— directs the operation of the computer
— receives data and instructions and sends them to the correct unit for processing
— indicates order in which operations are performed
— receives final results and sends them to output device
— usually implemented with arithmetic unit

Arithmetic Unit

— does all calculations and data transformations
— performs logical operations
— usually implemented with control unit

MEMORY

— where data, permanent and nonpermanent instructions, and results are stored until needed
— logical memory is of two types:

    1.   ROM (Read Only Memory) where instructions are permanently stored, for example, the BASIC language; in general you can't write into it, just read

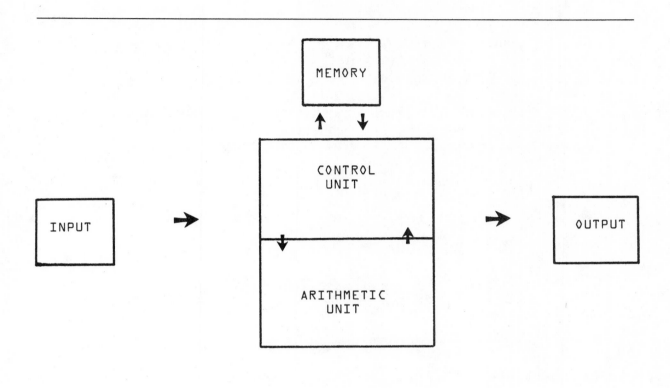

Figure 1.1: Schematic Diagram of the Major Parts of the Computer

from it; is nonvolatile, that is, not lost when the machine is turned off.
2.   RAM (Random Access Memory) where data and instructions the user inputs are stored; is volatile, that is, is wiped out when computer is turned off.

INPUT PORTS

— information (data and instructions) goes into the computer from the user via input ports
— may be such devices as keyboard, cassette, punched cards, disks, graphic pads, light pens, modems, sensors, and so on

OUTPUT PORTS

— results and data flow to outside world via output ports
— may be such devices as line printer, plotter, video screen, disks, modems, punched cards, and so on

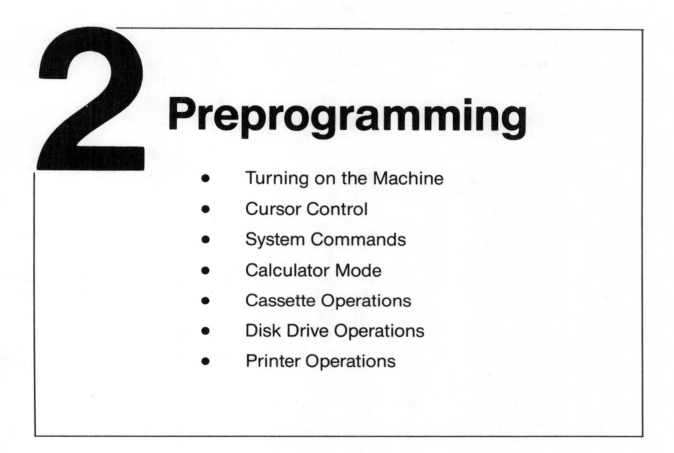

2 Preprogramming

- Turning on the Machine
- Cursor Control
- System Commands
- Calculator Mode
- Cassette Operations
- Disk Drive Operations
- Printer Operations

In this chapter, we discuss the basic operations of a microcomputer that a teacher or student must know in order to begin using a microcomputer. These operations include turning on the machine, control and use of the flashing cursor, using the microcomputer as a calculator, and the operation of the cassette recorder. Additional sections on printer and disk drive operation are included at the end of this chapter.

TURNING ON THE MACHINE

When the 16 mm projector was first introduced into the classroom, some teachers were apprehensive about its use. They were unsure of how to turn it on, how to load the film, how to rewind the film, and what to do if the projector malfunctioned in the middle of the film. Through practice, most teachers have found using the projector to actually be very simple.

The microcomputer is also simple to use. In some ways it is easier to use than a movie projector. A five-year old can load a tape and run a microcomputer; the same five-year old probably could not load and run a 16 mm projector.

When the 16 mm projector is plugged in, it will do nothing until it is told to do so by the user. Film must be loaded into the projector first; this is not an easy task if done manually. To run the film you need to "tell" the projector to do this by turning the switch ahead one position. However, you still won't see a picture because you must also tell the projector to turn on the light. Again you tell it by means of the switch, that is, turning the switch forward another position.

Like the projector, the microcomputer must also be told what to do, but the method is much simpler. First, look at the back of your PET. There you will find the power switch, a fuse, a power cord, and some holes to access the microcomputer with other devices such as the cassette recorder. On the Commodore 64 and the Vic 20, these are on the right-hand side as well as the back.

Find the cassette port. It is on the left-hand side as you face the rear of the PET. On the C64 and Vic 20, it is the second port from the right as you face the back. Carefully plug in the cassette recorder; it will only go in one way. Now plug in your microcomputer. NEVER plug in the cassette recorder if the microcomputer is on. (It is assumed that your C64 or Vic 20 is already connected to a video. If not, check the user's guide that came with the computer for the proper connection.)

To turn on the microcomputer, simply reach behind it with your left hand and turn on the power rocker switch. The power switch is on the right side of the computer on the C64 and the Vic 20. Wait a second. The PET will make a tinkling sound so you know it is actually on. You'll also see a message appear on the screen. If you are using a "Fat Forty," a 4032 PET with a 12″ screen, Figure 2.1 illustrates the message you will see. We will be using a 4032 PET microcomputer as the reference in the rest of this book. A similar message will appear on other PETs, the C64, and Vic 20.

What does this message mean?

Line 1: This means you are using a Commodore microcomputer that is equipped with the language BASIC.
Line 2: This tells you how much free memory you have for your use.
Line 3: This tells you the microcomputer is ready for you to do something, for example, RUN a program, type in a program, and so on.

```
### COMMODORE BASIC 4.0 ###
31727 BYTES FREE

READY

■
```

Figure 2.1: Message upon Powering Up

Line 4: This is the blinking cursor. It tells you where the microcomputer will begin printing on the screen.

To summarize:

1. Plug in cassette recorder on back of microcomputer.
2. Plug in the cord.
3. Turn the power switch on.

CURSOR CONTROL

The flashing square is called the cursor. The cursor indicates to the user the exact location on the screen where printing will appear when something is typed in. Controlling the position of the cursor is important in editing your program text. There are 4 keys that control the cursor's position; the keys are located on the calculator pad (Figure 2.2) located on the right-hand side of the keyboard of the PET. These keys are located on the top and bottom right-hand side of the keyboard on the C64 and Vic 20.

When a cursor key is pressed, the cursor will perform the directive on the bottom of the cursor control key. If the SHIFT key is held down when a cursor control key is pressed, the cursor will perform the directive on the top of the key. Practice will help you become familiar with the cursor control keys.

THE CLR-HOME KEY

Turn the microcomputer on. If you have just turned it on, the cursor will be flashing just under the word READY. Press the CLR-HOME key. Where did the cursor go? It went to the top left of the screen. This is the "home" position of the screen. If you press this key, the cursor will always return to this same position no matter where it was located before you pressed the key.

Now hold down the SHIFT key as you press the CLR-HOME key. What happens? What does CLR on the key stand for?

THE DELETE KEY

Now that you have cleared the screen, type in your name from the keyboard. Now press the INST-DEL key once. What happens? Now press and hold down the INST-DEL key. What happens? This key erases or deletes anything left of the cursor. It deletes one letter at a time and can be held down if you wish to delete more than a couple letters of your text. On older PETs and other types of computers, you may have to continually hit this key to have it repeat.

THE CURSOR DOWN KEY

Type in three or four lines of something onto the screen. (For the time being, ignore any error message you might get after each line when pressing the RETURN key.) Press the CRSR ↓ key and hold it down. Watch the screen. What happens? This is called scrolling and can be used if you wish to have something at the bottom of the screen move higher up to the top.

THE CURSOR UP KEY

Turn the machine off then on again. Hold down the SHIFT key as you press the CRSR ↑ key. Continue until the cursor is in the home position. What happens once you reach the home position?

THE CURSOR RIGHT KEY

Now press the CRSR → key. What happens? Now press the same key and hold it down. What happens?

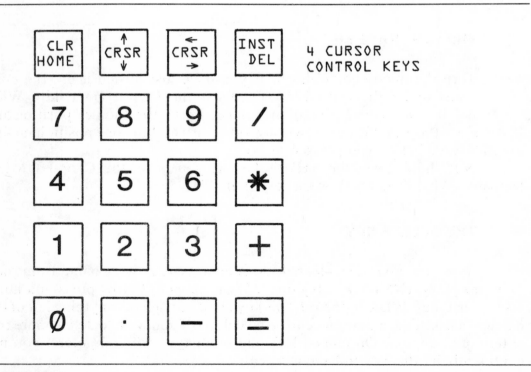

Figure 2.2: Calculator Pad

THE CURSOR LEFT KEY

What do you expect to happen if you hold down the SHIFT key as you press the CRSR ← key? Try it to confirm your guess.

THE INSERT KEY

This key probably causes the most confusion of all the cursor control keys. However, it is very valuable when editing text and therefore worth the effort to learn its proper use.

Clear the screen (by holding down the SHIFT and pressing the CLR-HOME key) and type in the word "GET." Now suppose that you wish to change GET to GREET. You could type the whole word over. However, if this word were in the middle of a line you would have to retype the entire line in order to get the correct spacing. By using the INST-DEL key you will be able to insert letters without having to retype anything.

Move the cursor back to the E in GET by using the correct cursor control key. Hold down the SHIFT key and press the INST-DEL twice. What happens? There should be two spaces now inserted between the G and T so that the word now looks like G   ET. Now type in RE and move the cursor past the T.

Cursor control is not difficult, requires some practice, and is a very efficient way of making corrections or changes to the text on the screen.

Exercises:

1. Type in MICROMPUTER.
   Make the appropriate spelling correction.
2. Type in BASIC PROGRAMMING.
   Press the RETURN key (ignore any error message).
   Reposition the cursor to make the following corrections.
   Remove the MING to change the word to PROGRAM.
   Delete the word BASIC.
3. Now change PROGRAM to ASSEMBLY LANGUAGE PROGRAMMING.
4. Type in GET.
5. Change GET to GREAT!

SYSTEM COMMANDS

If you have the word GREAT! on the screen, press the RETURN key. What happens?

This message means that you haven't used a word that was preprogrammed into the microcomputer's permanent memory, ROM. (See section on the parts of the computer or glossary.)

In order for the microcomputer system to work you must type in a word that it understands. These words are listed below and a detailed explanation of how to use them can be found in the succeeding sections and in Chapter 6.

Pet System Commands

LOAD   (loads a program from a tape or disk into the computer)

RUN   (tells the computer to run a program)

NEW   (wipes out present program in computer)

CONT   (continues a program if you drop out of it)

LIST   (lists out the lines of a program)

SAVE   (copies a program from the computer to a tape or disk)

VERIFY   (verifies that the program copied to the tape or disk is the same as that in the computer)

CALCULATOR MODE

Your microcomputer can be used as a calculator. Any time the word READY is displayed on the screen you can perform a mathematical calculation.

In order to perform these calculations, the following points should be kept in mind:

1. Computers follow order of operations as in mathematics; that is, operations in brackets are done first, then exponents, then multiplication and division left to right, and finally addition and subtraction left to right.
2. The word PRINT (or its short form "?") goes before the operation and tells the computer to print the answer to the calculation onto the screen, for example, ? 4 + 5.
3. The equal sign " = " is never used.
4. Each left bracket must have a corresponding right bracket or an error message will result.
5. The signs of operation are
   + for addition
   − for subtraction
   * for multiplication
   / for division
   ↑ for powers

6. No signs can be assumed, for example, 4a must be typed in as 4 * a, and, for example, 2a (3a) must be typed in as 2 * a * (3 * a). Brackets may be optional.

Exercises:

1. Type in the following calculations. Remember to hit RETURN after typing in each one. What answer is given by the microcomputer?

    a. ? 4 + 5
    b. ? 5 − 3
    c. ? 2 * 3
    d. ? 2 / 3
    e. ? 2 ↑ 3
    f. ? (2 + 3) * 5

2. Type each of the following correctly into the microcomputer and record the solution given. Remember, the computer does not assume multiplication where there is no sign.

    a. 35 − 7(4)
    b. 4(3 − 1) + 2
    c. $\dfrac{36}{5 + 1}$
    d. $5^2 − 2(4 + 3)$
    e. 2(6) − 3
    f. 25 − 20 / 4

CASSETTE OPERATIONS

There are three system commands that are used with the cassette recorder: SAVE, LOAD, and VERIFY. Each of these will be discussed briefly here. A summary of this information can be found in the section SYSTEM COMMANDS.

SAVE

This command puts information from the microcomputer onto the tape so the user has a permanent copy. Remember what you type into the microcomputer is volatile, that is, when you turn off the machine it disappears. If this information couldn't be saved on tape it would have to be typed in each time the microcomputer was turned on.

To save your program on a tape:

1. Insert a blank tape into the cassette recorder (or wind to a blank area on a tape).
2. Type SAVE and press RETURN or type SAVE "name of your program" and press RETURN.
    for example, SAVE "MY MATH PROGRAM" (press RETURN).
3. Follow the instructions given on the screen.

In step two, you have given the program the name "MY MATH PROGRAM." You can name your program anything up to a maximum of sixteen characters. The microcomputer puts this name on the tape followed by the actual program.

The following is the sequence of steps that appear on the screen (T = you type in; R = response of the microcomputer):

T: SAVE "MY MATH PROGRAM"
R: PRESS PLAY AND RECORD ON TAPE #1
R: OK (This occurs after you push the buttons on the tape drive.)
R: WRITING (or SAVING) (Your program is being written on the tape. Be patient here; it usually takes a few minutes.)
R: READY (The microcomputer is finished.)

Note that on the C64 the screen will become blank after you press the keys on the recorder; when your program is completely saved, a READY will appear on the screen.

There is a small blank gap between programs saved on a tape because the PET writes a 7 to 10 second leader after it accepts the SAVE command from the keyboard.

VERIFY

Once you have saved a program, you want to be confident that the program you now have saved on tape is exactly the same as that which you have in the microcomputer. To check this, you use the command VERIFY.

To verify your program:

1. Rewind the tape to the point where you began to save your program.
2. Type VERIFY and press RETURN or type VERIFY "name of program" and press RETURN.
    for example, VERIFY "MY MATH PROGRAM" (press RETURN)
3. Follow the instructions given on the screen.

The following is the sequence of steps that appear on the screen of a PET. Similar responses appear on the C64 and Vic 20.

T: VERIFY "MY MATH PROGRAM"
R: PRESS PLAY ON TAPE #1

```
R:  OK
R:  SEARCHING
R:  FOUND "MY MATH PROGRAM"
R:  VERIFYING
R:  OK
R:  READY
```

The above happens if your tape is an exact copy of your program in the microcomputer. If it is not, you will see a "?VERIFY ERROR" in place of the OK. In this case you begin the SAVE process again until you get an exact copy.

LOAD

Now that you have saved and verified your program, you can put it back into the computer with the LOAD command.

To load your program:

1. Rewind your tape.
2. Type LOAD and press RETURN or
   type LOAD "MY MATH PROGRAM" and press RETURN.
   (If you type only LOAD, the computer will load the first complete program on the tape that it encounters.)
3. Follow the instructions given on the screen.

The following is the sequence of steps that appear on the screen of a PET:

```
T:  LOAD "MY MATH PROGRAM"
R:  PRESS PLAY ON TAPE #1
R:  OK
R:  FOUND "MY MATH PROGRAM"
R:  LOADING
R:  READY
```

You are now ready to RUN your program. This is accomplished by typing in the word RUN and pressing the RETURN key.

Please note that the microcomputer does not check to see which keys have been pressed on the cassette recorder. It assumes that you have pressed the correct keys.

DISK DRIVE OPERATIONS

If you don't have a disk drive for the computer that you are using, then you can skip this section; but consider getting one since a disk drive makes loading and saving programs much easier and faster than a tape cassette.

This section will be kept short; it will show you how to load and list a disk directory and how to load from and save programs to a disk when using a PET. For further information you should consult your user's guide, the manual that came with the disk drive and the Test/Demo disk that was probably supplied.

The disk drive is connected to the second port from the tape port on the back of the computer. This configuration is shown on page 34 of the *PET/CBM Personal Computer Guide*.

The steps to loading a program from the disk using BASIC versions before 4.0 are as follows:

1. OPEN a logical file and device.
2. Initialize the drive(s).
3. LOAD and LIST the directory (optional).
4. LOAD the program from the specific drive.

To perform the above steps:

1. To open the logical file number to the disk drive
    TYPE: OPEN 1, 8, 15
2. To initialize the disk drive
    TYPE: PRINT #1, "I0" (0 is the disk drive number, use either 1 or 0)
    To initialize both drives
    TYPE: PRINT #1, "I"
3. To load the directory
    TYPE: LOAD "$0", 8
    where the 0 is the drive number and the 8 is the device number. The computer
    will respond with READY; then type LIST
4. To load a program from the disk
    TYPE: LOAD "0: program name", 8
    where the 0 is again the drive number and the 8 is the device number
5. To save a program on the disk
    TYPE: SAVE "0: program name", 8

(Notice that the syntax is the same as it was for loading except that the word SAVE is used instead of LOAD. However, make sure if you are saving a program that the lines are open and the drives initialized.)

PRINTER OPERATIONS

If you don't have a printer for the computer that you are using, then you can skip this section; but, consider getting one since a printer is one of the more useful devices that can be added to your machine. Documents of all types can be printed out as well as listings of programs. "Hard copies" of information may sometimes be necessary. For example, if you are a teacher and you need a copy of your class and their marks for the school administration, then you can quickly get a copy if you have a printer.

This section will be kept short; it will show one way to get a listing of a computer program onto the printer and how to print directly to the printer when using a PET. For further information you should consult the user's guide and the manual that came with the printer.

The printer is connected to the second port from the tape port if you are using the printer alone. Otherwise, it is connected to the disk drive. The configurations are shown in the *PET/CBM Personal Computer Guide* on pages 41-42.

To list a program onto the printer:

1.   LOAD a program into the computer.
2.   Type in the following line exactly as printed:
     OPEN 5, 4: CMD 5: LIST
3.   Press RETURN (Your program will begin to list onto the printer.)
4.   After the listing is finished type PRINT #5: CLOSE 5.

The OPEN statement opens an output line to the printer. This is analogous to a road with a green light. The 5 following this can be any number from 1 to 255 as long as the number in the OPEN, CMD, and CLOSE statements is the same. The CMD directs data to be sent to the printer. The LIST statement lists the program step by step as it would on the screen only the listing is to the printer. Always remember the CLOSE statement at the end.

To print something directly to the printer:
Here you use the PRINT statement instead of the LIST. Try these examples.

1.   Type OPEN 5, 4: CMD 5: PRINT "COMPUTERS ARE GREAT!"
     result: READY
     COMPUTERS ARE GREAT!
2.   Type PRINT "I LOVE MY PET"
     result:, READY
     I LOVE MY PET
3.   Type PRINT #5: CLOSE 5

3 BASIC Programming

- PRINT, GOTO, and REM
- Variables: LET Statement
- Built-In Functions
- INPUT
- READ-DATA
- IF-THEN
- Counter and Adder
- AND OR
- FOR-NEXT
- Nested Loops
- Flags
- Time Delay and Flashing Screen
- ON-GOTO
- Random Numbers
- PEEK and POKE
- GOSUB

1. PRINT, GOTO, AND REM

The PRINT statement tells the computer to print something onto the screen. This could be words, numbers, spaces, or graphics. The ? is a short form for PRINT.

Whatever is to be printed onto the screen, including spaces and/or punctuation marks, must be in quotation marks. (An exception to this is if you want the value of a variable to be printed. This will be discussed in Sample Program 1.3 and in the next section.) If you want actual quotation marks to be printed, an apostrophe in place of the quotation marks will have to be used.

SAMPLE PROGRAM 1.1

(Type this and all following sample programs *exactly* as shown and then RUN them. To run them, type RUN and press RETURN. Observe what happens and answer any questions. Figure 3.1 gives an explanation of each part of this program.)

```
10 PRINT "WHAT IS YOUR NAME?"
20 END
```

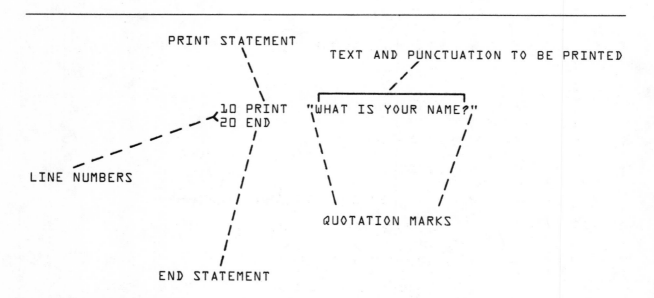

Figure 3.1:   The Parts of Sample Program 3.1

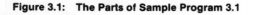

Questions

1a. What is printed when you RUN this program?
 b. What part of line 10 is not printed on the screen?
2.   What do you think line 20 does?

Type NEW. This will clear the computer of any previous programs. *You should type this each time you begin a new program.*

SAMPLE PROGRAM 1.2

Use the shifted N, M, T, and Y keys to make the graphics of your rocket.

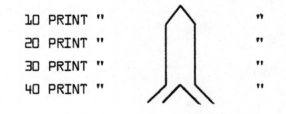

```
10 PRINT "          "
20 PRINT "          "
30 PRINT "          "
40 PRINT "          "
```

Question

3. What is printed?

Now add the line 100 GOTO 10 to your program and RUN it. (Notice that there is no PRINT in this line.)

Question

4. What happens?

(You can stop the program by pressing the RUN-STOP key.)

Line 100 tells the computer to branch back to line 10. The computer again then executes lines 10, 20, 30, and 40 sequentially.

Now add the following lines to your rocket program:

```
45 PRINT
50 PRINT
55 PRINT
60 PRINT
65 PRINT
70 PRINT
```

Question

5. What does an "empty" PRINT statement do?

Note that the computer puts statement lines in the correct numerical sequence regardless of the order in which they were typed.

SAMPLE PROGRAM 1.3

(Remember to type NEW to wipe out the rocket program.)

```
10  ? 10
20  ? "HELLO"
```

Questions

6. What type of punctuation encloses words?
7. Do numeric values (line 10) need quotation marks?

SAMPLE PROGRAM 1.4

```
5  REM USES OF COMMA, SEMICOLON, TAB
10 ? "HI", "HOW ARE YOU?"
20 ? "HI"; "HOW ARE YOU?"
30 ? "HI"; TAB (15); "HOW ARE YOU?"
```

Questions

8. What is the spacing difference between the use of the comma and the semicolon?
9. How would you change line 10 to insert a space between HI and HOW?
10. What does the TAB function do?
11. REM had no effect on the operation of the program. What then, do you think is its function?

SAMPLE PROGRAM 1.5

In this sample program:

R means that you press the OFF-RVS key (on C64 and Vic 20, press CTRL and RVS-ON keys).

CLR means that you press the SHIFT and CLR-HOME keys.

↓ means that you press the cursor down key.

→ means that you press the cursor right key.

```
10 ? "CLR"
20 ? "R ↓ ↓ ↓ ↓ ↓ → → → → → JOHN SMITH"
30 GOTO 30
```

Questions

12. What does the *CLR* do to the screen?
13. What color are the letters of the name?
14. What color is the background to the letters?
    (This is referred to as reverse video.)
15. What do you think is the purpose of line 30?

IMPORTANT POINTS TO REMEMBER

1. Quotation marks are necessary if you wish to use the PRINT statement for anything other than numbers or variables. (See next section on variables.)

2. All lines of a program must begin with a line number. The computer puts line numbers in numerical sequence regardless of the order in which you typed them.

3. A line like 30 GOTO 30 puts the computer in an endless loop. This line prevents the cursor and READY from appearing on the screen at the end of a program.

4. You can stop a program by pressing the RUN-STOP key.

5. The screen can be divided into 4 columns or fields by using the comma in PRINT statements.

6. Information can be run together in PRINT statements by using the semicolon.

7. Cursor control can be programmed into PRINT statements.

8. The PRINT statement and the OFF/RVS key can be used to put information on the screen in reverse mode. To switch back to normal mode, press OFF-RVS again (CTRL and RVS-OFF on the C64 and Vic 20) or RETURN.

9. The TAB function always tabs over from the left side of the screen.

10. Before you type in a new program, remember to type NEW to wipe out the previous program.

Exercises

1. Write a program to print a heart or any other graphic near the four corners of the screen.
2. Modify the above program to print your name near the four corners of the screen.
3. Modify the program again to print your name near the four corners of the screen and also to print your name in reverse field in the center of the screen.

---

2. VARIABLES: LET STATEMENT

One of the most valuable uses of the microcomputer is its ability to perform mathematical calculations accurately, repetitively, and with amazing speed. In these calculations, variables that represent number values are often used.

There are two types of variables: numeric and nonnumeric. Nonnumeric variables are also called string variables. Variable names can be any length, however, only the first two letters are used by the computer when distinguishing between variables. For example, WI, WIDTH, WI1, and WI2 are *not* distinct variable names because they all have the same first two letters. If the variable is a string variable, the first two letters and the $ are significant. For example, NA$ is significant for the string variable NAME$.

Variable names cannot contain the same first letters as a built-in function. (See section on built-in functions.) For example, LEN is a built-in function, therefore no variable can begin with LE. Variables names may contain digits but not begin with digits. For example, H1, H2B, N3 are valid: however, 1H, 2HB, 3N are not valid names.

When the computer solves an equation for an unknown variable, this unknown must be on the left-hand side of the equals sign. In calculations, the value of the right-hand side of the equation is assigned to the left-hand side.

$$Y = 5 + 2 - 3$$

The value 4 is assigned to Y.

The signs of operations are $+$ for addition, $-$ for subtraction, $*$ for multiplication, $/$ for division, and $\uparrow$ followed by the exponent for powers. Other useful built-in functions are SQR for square root, INT for integer rounding, and ABS for absolute value. The expression $\uparrow$ .5 can also be used for square root. (See the next section for a more in-depth discussion of these built-in functions.)

The order in which the computer performs these operations is the same as in mathematics:

Brackets
Exponents
Multiplication and division left to right
Addition and subtraction left to right

The LET statement can be used to assign a value to a variable . The term LET is optional on Commodore computers. Other computers (Timex-Sinclair 1000) require it. For example, A = 5 is as acceptable as LET A = 5.

SAMPLE PROGRAM 2.1

```
10  REM THIS PROGRAM SHOWS THE USE OF VARIABLES
20  LET A = 5
30  B = 10
40  C = B − A
50  LET D = B/A
60  E = B * A
70  F1 = B ↑ 2
80  G = G + 1
90  NAME$ = "ALBERT EINSTEIN"
100  LET E1$ = "E = M*C ↑ 2"
110  PRINT NAME$; "  DISCOVERED "; E1$
120  PRINT C
130  PRINT D
140  PRINT E
150  PRINT F1
160  PRINT B+A
170  PRINT G
```

Questions

1. What is the last character in a string variable?
2. What must enclose nonnumeric data?
3. If a variable is not enclosed in quotation marks in a PRINT statement (for example, line 120), what is printed?
4. What does the LET statement do?
5. Is the LET statement necessary?
6. How would B^3 be shown in a computer program?
7. Since G in line 80 has not been given a value, that is, has not been "initialized," what value does the computer automatically assign to it?

8. Correct each of the following statements:
    a. X = +2(+3)
    b. N1 = "ISAAC NEWTON"
    c. LET 4B = 20
    d. K = A × B
    e. ASTRONOMER$ = KEPLER

Exercises

1. Write a program that will calculate the circumference and area of a circle whose diameter is 4 cm. (Note the π key on the keyboard.)

2. Your savings account balance is $933.00. You make 3 withdrawals of $45, $150, and $227. You make two deposits of $200 and $100. Write a program that will print out your name using a string variable and determine and print out your new balance.

3. Your asphalt driveway is 12 ft. × 35 ft. You need 3 cans of asphalt sealer at $16.99 each to seal it. Write a program to calculate the area of the driveway and the total price of the sealer and print it out as follows:

THE DRIVEWAY IS 12 BY 35 (In your program, use a variable for these values instead of the actual value.)
THE AREA OF THE DRIVEWAY IS (ANSWER)
(SPACE)
ASPHALT SEALER WILL COST (ANSWER)

---

3. BUILT-IN FUNCTIONS

The microcomputer has several built-in functions that may be needed in mathematical calculations. Only a few of the available functions will be discussed here.

SQR is the square root function. The number for which the square root is desired is put in parentheses immediately following the letters SQR, for example, SQR(16). Square root can also be calculated by using $\uparrow$ .5, for example, 16 $\uparrow$ .5.

ABS is the absolute value function. By means of this function, negative numbers become positive and positive numbers remain positive.

INT is the integer function. It rounds off decimal numbers, either positive or negative, into whole numbers or integers. It is important to note that the integer function on Commodore computers rounds *DOWN* to the next lowest number. Some other computers round to the nearest integer.

SAMPLE PROGRAM 3.1

Run this program and note the rounding of each number.

```
10 REM THIS PROGRAM DEMONSTRATES THE INTEGER FUNC-
TION
20 C = INT (7.777)
30 D = INT (−7.777)
40 E = INT (7.111)
50 F = INT (−7.111)
60 PRINT C, D, E, F
```

Each time something is stored in the computer, a certain amount of memory space is used up. A numerical value, for example, 34, takes up more space than if "34" is stored as a string. (Only numerical values can be used in calculations.) The function VAL will take a number stored as a string and change it into a numerical value.

SAMPLE PROGRAM 3.2

Run and observe how the VAL function works.

```
10 REM THIS PROGRAM DEMONSTRATES THE VAL FUNCTION
20 A$ = "34"
30 PRINT A$
40 B = VAL (A$)
50 PRINT B
60 PRINT B + 0
```

Functions are reserved words; no variable may start out with the same two letters as a function. Other useful functions not discussed here include LOG for logarithm, EXP for exponent, COS for cosine, SIN for sine. Functions that have been previously discussed or will be discussed later include TAB, RND, PEEK, TIME, and TIME$.

Questions

1. What would be the result of the following? Check your answers using the calculator mode of the computer.
   a. ABS (−7.45)
   b. SQR(25)
   c. INT (−7.5)
   d. ABS(+7.45)
   e. INT (7.9)
2. Write these as they would be typed on the computer and the answers that will result.
   a. ABS (−5) $\sqrt{16}$
   b. (3²) ($\sqrt{100}$)
   c. 4(6)+INT(−6.9)
   d. ABS(−6) (2²) ($\sqrt{9}$)
   e. 4 × 5 ÷ $\sqrt{100}$
3. Write a three line program which will contain a remark, declare the number 24 as a string, then change it from a string to a numerical value, add it to 6, and print out the answer.

4. INPUT

The INPUT statement causes the computer to print a ? then wait until information is typed in by the user. It is an "interactive" statement between computer and user.

SAMPLE PROGRAM 4.1

```
10 ? "HELLO. MY NAME IS PET. WHAT'S YOURS?"
20 INPUT A$
30 ? "NICE TO MEET YOU "; A$
```

When you run the program, the computer stops at line 20 and waits. It will wait forever, as long as the power is turned on, or until you type in something, for example your name. The program continues after you have typed in the information and pressed RETURN.

The information typed in by the user is stored in a memory location called A$. Remember the symbol $ denotes that the information is a string of letters. Therefore, the computer will treat your answer as a string of characters and not as a numerical value.

The following program uses the INPUT statement to accept two numbers from the keyboard and then adds the two numbers together to get a result.

SAMPLE PROGRAM 4.2

```
10 ? "THIS PROGRAM ADDS TOGETHER ANY TWO NUMBERS
THAT ARE TYPED IN BY THE USER."
20 ? "WHAT TWO NUMBERS DO YOU WISH TO ADD?"
30 INPUT A, B
40 LET C = A + B
50 ? C
```

Lines 20 and 30 in this program can be combined to read:

```
20 INPUT "WHAT TWO NUMBERS DO YOU WISH TO ADD?"; A, B
```

Questions

1. What is the difference between A and A$?
2. Combine lines 10 and 20 in Sample Program 4.1 into one statement line.
3. Run Sample Program 4.2 and hit RETURN without typing in any data. What happens?

Exercises

1. Change Sample Program 4.2 to multiply any two numbers.
2. Modify line 50 in Sample Program 4.2 so that the output will read "THE ANSWER IS" and then print the answer all on the same line.
3. Write a program that will ask for a person's name, street address, city, and postal code, and then print it out on the screen like an address label on an envelope.

---

5. READ-DATA

Another method of putting data, either numeric or strings, into a program is by using the READ-DATA statements. A READ statement assigns variable names to actual data contained in the DATA statement.

Data can be in the form of integers, decimals, floating point or E-notation, and strings. DATA statements may not contain variables and arithmetic operations including fractions or functions.

SAMPLE PROGRAM 5.1

```
10  REM THIS PROGRAM SHOWS THE USE OF READ-DATA
20  READ NAME$, S1, S2, S3, S4
30  DATA "JOE SMITH", 90, 56, 73, 83
40  AVERAGE = (S1+S2+S3+S4)/4
50  PRINT "THE TERM AVERAGE FOR  ";NAME$;"  IS"; AVERAGE
```

Questions

1. What is the purpose of this program?
2. How are variable names separated in the READ statement?
3. How are data separated in the DATA statement?
4. How are string variables indicated in the READ statement?
5. What must enclose nonnumeric data?

SAMPLE PROGRAM 5.2

```
10  REM TERM AVERAGES FOR STUDENTS
20  READ N$, S1 ,S2, S3, S4
30  AV = (S1+S2+S3+S4)/4
40  PRINT "THE AVERAGE FOR ";N$;"  IS"; AV
50  GOTO 20
60  DATA "JOE SMITH", 90, 56, 73, 82
70  DATA "MARY JONES", 100, 100, 100, 100
80  DATA "JOHN WHITE", 54, 63, 72, 77, "JANE BLACK", 81, 60, 70, 43
```

Questions

6a. Compare the position of the DATA statements in Sample Programs 5.1 and 5.2. Does the position matter?
 b. Change line 60 to line 5 and rerun this program. What happens?
7. After the first name and average are printed, what becomes N$?
8. What happens when all available data are used up?

Most programmers put all DATA statements at the end of the program; there, they are easy to locate and extra data can always be added. Others, however, pair up the READ statement with its appropriate DATA statement. Whatever the location, DATA statements are always read in consecutive order, left to right. A pointer moves from one DATA to the next, each time a READ statement is encountered, to the end of the DATA.

By adding a RESTORE statement to a program, the pointer to the next DATA items can be reset to the beginning of the DATA list. If, for some reason, the data had to be read more than once, a RESTORE statement saves the programmer from having to type in the data lists several times. The RESTORE statement stands by itself in a program line, for example:

20 RESTORE

In summary, data, then, can be placed in a program by three methods: by assigning values to variables with or without the optional LET statement; by means of the INPUT statement; and by means of the READ-DATA statement.

Exercises

1. Write a program that will read in your name, age, hair color, eye color, favorite food and sports car and then print it out as follows:

MY NAME IS (name) AND I AM (age) YEARS OLD.

I HAVE (color) HAIR AND (color) EYES.

MY FAVORITE FOOD IS (food) AND I WOULD LOVE TO OWN A (car).

2. Write a program that will read in the name of the school subject and time, the name of 3 students and their last 3 test scores, and will print them out as follows:

TEST SCORES FOR   (subject) AT (time).

NAME	TEST SCORES	AVERAGE
JOHN DOE (etc.)	80 90 73	

3. Now add one more student's name and test scores to the above program.

4. Write a program that will read in a person's name, savings account number, beginning balance, 2 deposits, and 2 withdrawals, and will print out a statement as follows:

JOHN DOE   #32-40089

BEGINNING BALANCE: $

DEPOSITS   WITHDRAWALS

_____   _____

_____   _____

FINAL BALANCE: $

6. IF-THEN

The IF-THEN statement used in combination with relational operators allows the computer to compare one value or string to another and then branch into one of two paths, depending on whether the statement is true or false. If the statement is true, the command after "THEN" is performed; if it is false, the computer simply proceeds onto the next statement. Commands often used after the "THEN" include PRINT, GOTO, and GOSUB.

The relational operators are:

= equals
<> does not equal
> greater than
< less than
>= greater than or equal to
<= less than or equal to

SAMPLE PROGRAM 6.1

```
10  REM THIS PROGRAM TELLS WHETHER A VALUE IS
20  REM GREATER THAN, LESS THAN, OR EQUAL TO 10
30  INPUT "TYPE ANY NUMBER INTO THE COMPUTER"; X
40  IF X <> 10 THEN GOTO 70
50  PRINT X; "EQUALS 10"
```

```
60  END
70  PRINT X; "DOES NOT EQUAL 10"
80  IF X > 10 THEN GOTO 110
90  PRINT X; "IS LESS THAN 10"
100 END
110 PRINT X; "IS GREATER THAN 10"
```

Questions

1. What happens in the program if line 40 is true?
2. What happens in the program if line 40 is false?
3. Observe lines 40 and 80. Describe the transfer of control when the statement is false.
4. What is accomplished by lines 60 and 100?

The same relational operators can be used with strings. The letter A is less than the letter B; B is less than C; A is also less than AA; AA is less than AAA; Z is less than ZZ; and so on. Note that unlike variable names, the microcomputer will look beyond the first two letters when comparing strings.

SAMPLE PROGRAM 6.2

```
10 REM RELATIONAL OPERATORS USED WITH STRINGS
20 INPUT "TYPE IN ANY TWO WORDS"; W1$, W2$
30 IF W1$ < W2$ THEN GOTO 60
40 PRINT W2$; " COMES ALPHABETICALLY BEFORE "; W1$
50 GOTO 70
60 PRINT W1$; " COMES ALPHABETICALLY BEFORE "; W2$
70 INPUT "DO YOU WANT TO DO THIS AGAIN? (YES OR NO)"; ANS$
80 IF ANS$ = "YES" THEN GOTO 20
90 END
```

Questions

5. What happens if line 30 is true?
6. What happens if line 30 is false?

7. Circle the "lesser" of the following pairs:
   a. CAT   CAB
   b. CAT   CATS
   c. MMM   MMMM
   d. DDDD   DADDY
8. Change line 30 in Sample Program 6.2 so there is a PRINT command with a GOTO. Eliminate or add any other lines as needed.

Exercises

1. Write a program that will read in the following numbers and print only those numbers that are positive in value. The numbers are $-2.5, 0, 10, 2.345, -7, 6, +22$ (Note: You will get an out-of-data message at the end of your program.)

2. Write a program to print a "*" 80 times or 2 rows (40 times on a Vic 20) across the screen using an IF-THEN statement, not a FOR-NEXT loop. (Note: You will need to use a counter with this program; see next section counters and adders.)

---

7. COUNTER AND ADDER

The microcomputer is an ideal device for counting and adding up numbers. The counter is often used to keep track of the number of iterations of a procedure being done; the adder is used to keep track of an ongoing sum as the program continues.

The microcomputer's central processing unit, the microprocessor, can address a large amount of memory. In order to do this, the microcomputer must keep track of where each memory location is. This is done automatically; the user does not have to remember.

Each memory cell has a name that we assign to it as we assign variables to certain values. For example, suppose we LET X = 10. We have assigned some memory location the value of 10; we call the memory location X. Instead of reading this as X equals 10, we should read: X is assigned the value of 10. It doesn't matter where in the actual memory address X carrying the value of 10 is located. The microcomputer knows where it is. When we want to refer to this value later in a program, we need only to refer to the name of that memory location that we assigned, in this case X.

$$X \qquad\qquad = \qquad\qquad 10$$
name of memory location   value in that location

This step assigns the value 10 to the variable X; this step is referred to as "initializing" and must be done as the first step in the actual counting procedure. During this process of counting, 1 is added each time to the preceding value of X to assign X a new value.

SAMPLE PROGRAM 7.1

10 REM THIS PROGRAM COUNTS FROM 1 TO INFINITY
20 REM AS LONG AS THE PROGRAM IS RUNNING
30 X = 0 (This line "initializes" X to the value 0.)
40 X = X+1 (This line adds 1 to the value in location X and replaces the old value of X with this new sum.)
50 PRINT X (This will print the new value of X.)
60 GOTO 40 (This goes back to the counter in line 40 where 1 more is added and the new sum stored.)

Questions

1. Why doesn't line 60 say GOTO 30 where the actual program starts?
2. Change line 40 so that the program counts by 2s; by halves.

The adder is very similar to the counter but here we want to keep track of the ongoing sum of the numbers we are counting. For example, if you are counting from 1 to 5 and wish to know the sum of the numbers from 1 to 5, you will need a counter to count from 1 to 5 and an adder to add 1 + 2, store this in memory, then add 3, store this new sum and continue this procedure until the program has reached 5.

Two memory locations will be necessary, one to keep track of the count, which we will call X, and the other to keep track of the sum, which we will call S. Suppose that we start with 0 and count by 1s. The X memory cell will become progressively 1, 2, 3, 4, 5, and so on. The adder then adds each value of X to value in the memory cell we called S. The initial value is 0. The microcomputer acts on the values in the following manner:

NEW S = OLD S + NEW X

The program starts with the current value in S, adds the new value of X, and stores this new sum in S.

SAMPLE PROGRAM 7.2

```
10  REM ADD THE NUMBERS FROM 1 TO 10 AND PRINT THE SUM
19  REM A COLON—AS IN LINE 20—ALLOWS MULTIPLE STATE-
MENTS ON ONE LINE
20  X = 0: S = 0
30  X = X+1
40  S = S+X
50  IF X = 10 THEN GOTO 70
60  GOTO 30
70  PRINT S
80  END
```

Questions

3. Which line initializes the value of X and S?
4. Put remarks with lines 30 to 80 to explain what each does.

A way to understand what is happening in Sample Program 7.2 is to write out a counter and adder table for the program (Figure 3.2) that shows the value in X and S each time one iteration of the program is complete.

X	0	1	2	3	4	5	6	7	8	9	10
S	0	1	3	6	10	15	21	28	36	45	55

Figure 3.2: Counter and Adder Table

SAMPLE PROGRAM 7.3

```
10 REM
20 X = 0: S = 0
30 X = X+5
40 S = S+X
50 PRINT S
60 IF X = 20 THEN GOTO 80
70 GOTO 30
80 END
```

Questions

5. Put an appropriate REMark in line 10.
6. Write a counter-adder table for this program.

EXERCISES

1. Write a program to count from 10 to 20 and print out both the values of the counting numbers and each sum.

2. Write a program to count the numbers from 5 to 15 and print only the last number, that is, 15.

3. Write a program that will show the names of students on the left-hand side of the screen and then allow you as the teacher to input a mark beside each name. The program should then calculate the average of each set of data, that is, the class average.

4. Write a program that will print a simple calculation problem on the screen and give the student three chances to answer the question. If the student cannot get the correct answer after three tries, the computer will give it to him. Include PRINT statements that will indicate clearly whether the student got the correct answer.

8. AND OR

Often it is sufficient to have only one of two conditions true in order for a statement to be executed; this is the case with the logical OR statement. In other circumstances, several conditions must be true for the statement to be executed; this is the case when the logical AND is used.

SAMPLE PROGRAM 8.1

```
10 REM THIS PROGRAM SHOWS THE USE OF THE LOGICAL
"AND"
20 REM THIS PROGRAM WILL TELL IN WHICH QUADRANT OF A
GRAPH
25 REM AN ORDERED PAIR OF NUMBERS IS LOCATED
30 INPUT "TYPE IN 2 NUMBERS, EITHER POSITIVE OR NEGA-
TIVE"; X,Y
40 IF X > 0 AND Y > 0 THEN PRINT "YOUR NUMBER IS IN THE
FIRST QUADRANT": GOTO 100
50 IF X < 0 AND Y > 0 THEN PRINT "YOUR NUMBER IS IN THE
SECOND QUADRANT": GOTO 100
60 IF X < 0 AND Y < 0 THEN PRINT "YOUR NUMBER IS IN THE
THIRD QUADRANT": GOTO 100
70 IF X > 0 AND Y < 0 THEN PRINT "YOUR NUMBER IS IN THE
FOURTH QUADRANT": GOTO 100
80 IF X = 0 AND Y = 0 THEN PRINT "YOUR NUMBER IS AT THE
ORIGIN": GOTO 100
90 PRINT "YOUR NUMBER IS ON AN AXIS"
100 END
```

Questions

1. What conditions have to be met to print "YOUR NUMBER IS AT THE ORIGIN" (line 80)?
2. What conditions would get you to line 90?
3. What is a ":" used for?
4. Add lines to this program (after line 90) that allow the user to reexecute the program again beginning with line 30. Change other lines as needed.

SAMPLE PROGRAM 8.2

Add these lines to the previous program.

Change GOTO 100 in lines 40, 50, 60, 70 to GOTO 140

```
90 REM THIS PART SHOWS THE LOGICAL "OR"
100 REM THIS PART TELLS WHETHER AN ORDERED PAIR IS ON
```

```
110  REM THE X OR Y AXIS
120  IF Y > 0 OR Y < 0 THEN PRINT "YOUR NUMBER IS ON THE Y
AXIS": GOTO 140
130  IF X > 0 OR X < 0 THEN PRINT "YOUR NUMBER IS ON THE X
AXIS": GOTO 140
140  END
```

Question

5. Under what circumstances would line 90 of this program be reached?

Exercises

1. To win the award in scientific geography, a student must have an average of 80 or above on tests and a grade of 80 or above on a notebook. Write a program that will read in the name and data on each of the following students and will print out only the names of the possible candidates.

NAME	TEST AVERAGE	NOTEBOOK GRADE
John Smith	64	81
Joe Jones	82	79
Mary Brown	93	84
Ann Black	75	90
Robert Grey	97	89

2. Write a program that will perform the same task as the previous program but in addition will first determine the test average of the students. Use the following data.

NAME	TEST SCORES	NOTEBOOK GRADE
Jennifer Grant	100, 73, 79	85
Mary Baker	54, 92, 84	80
Joe Kelly	63, 67, 83	79
Bill Adams	78, 79, 89	81

9. FOR-NEXT

Iterative, or circular, loops can be incorporated into a program by means of the FOR-NEXT statement. Looping in a program is a procedure where a certain part of the program is repeated a number of times, from beginning to end and then back to the beginning again, over and over in a circle or "loop." This looping was done in the rocket program by means of a GOTO statement (see PRINT section).

The programmer decides the number of times the loop should occur and builds an automatic end into the loop. If no end is built in, the loop will go on forever until the program is terminated by the user, as was the case with the rocket, or until the power goes off.

The FOR-NEXT statement looks as follows:

```
10  FOR I = 1 TO 25
20  PRINT "HI"
30  NEXT I
40  END
```

The FOR statement must always have an accompanying NEXT statement that succeeds it somewhere in the program. In the above four line program, line 10 tells the computer to do something 25 times; line 20 tells what that something is, namely to print the word "HI"; line 30 tells the computer to keep looping back to line 20 but to add 1 to the automatic counter each time HI is printed. When the automatic counter reaches 25 times, the computer will print "HI" one last time and then go onto line 40: Twenty-five HIs will have been printed.

SAMPLE PROGRAM 9.1A

```
10  REM LOOPING USING THE IF AND GOTO STATEMENTS
20  REM COUNT TO 10 AND STOP
30  X = X+1
40  PRINT X
50  IF X = 10 THEN 70
60  GOTO 30
70  END
```

SAMPLE PROGRAM 9.1B

```
10  REM LOOPING USING THE FOR-NEXT STATEMENT
20  REM COUNT TO 10 AND STOP
30  FOR X = 1 TO 10
```

```
40  PRINT X
50  NEXT X
60  END
```

Questions

1. Fill in the blanks about Sample Program 9.1 A:
   a. The program starts counting from _____ (line 30).
   b. It counts by _____ (line 30).
   c. It stops counting when X = _____.
   d. It prints the numbers from _____ to _____.
   e. The statement that sends the program through the loop is
      _____.
2. Fill in the blanks about sample program 9.1B:
   a. Line 30 tells the computer to start to count from _____
      and to continue to _____.
   b. Line 40 tells the computer to _____.
   c. Line 50 tells the computer to go to line _____ and to
      continue the count.
3. Write lines 30 to 50 of Sample Program 9.1B as one statement
   line. (Hint: use :)

In Sample Program 9.1A, we could have counted by 2s if line 30 were X = X+2. In a similar manner, we could count backwards of line 30 were X = X−2. In Sample program 9.1B, we can add the STEP statement to the FOR statement to indicate which increments we desire.

SAMPLE PROGRAM 9.2

```
10  REM USING THE FOR-NEXT AND STEP
20  FOR Y = 10 TO 50 STEP 2
30  PRINT Y
40  NEXT Y
```

Questions

4. Change line 20 so the counting is done in increments of 3.
5. Change line 20 so the counting is done backwards from 10 to 0.
6. Modify Sample Program 9.2 so that the program steps by ½.

Exercises

1. Write a program using the FOR-NEXT statement that counts from 15 to 25 in increments of 1 and prints out only the last number.

2. Write a program that counts backward from 30 to 20 and prints out all the numbers.

3. Write a program that will print a specific graphic character, for example a heart, across the screen 10 times.

4. Modify the above program so that the graphic is printed down the left hand side of the screen the same number of times.

5. Write a program to print out the 10 times table on the screen. (Hint: Use the variable from the FOR-NEXT statement in your PRINT statement.)

10. NESTED LOOPS

Nested loops are loops within loops. In order to work correctly and to avoid an error message on the screen, the loops must be written in the program in the proper format. Figure 3.3 shows the proper format of nested loops.

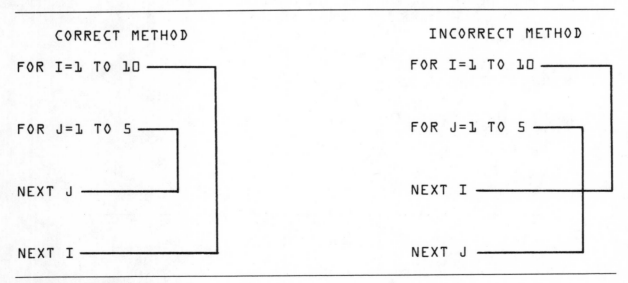

Figure 3.3: Format of Nested Loops

Suppose that you wanted to print a 6 × 4 rectangle on the screen in the upper left hand corner. You could do this by using a nested FOR-NEXT loop. The program and an explanation of each line follow.

SAMPLE PROGRAM 10.1

```
10 REM TO PRINT A 6 BY 4 RECTANGLE
20 FOR W=1 TO 4
30 FOR L=1 TO 6
40 PRINT  "■";
50 NEXT L
60 PRINT
70 NEXT W
80 END
```

Line 10: Tells what the program does but is not executed by the computer.

Lines 30 to 50: This is the inner loop that prints the graphic 6 times on a line. The ";" at the end of line 40 tells the computer to print the graphic on the same line.

Line 60: Prints a carriage return, so the cursor moves to the next line after printing the graphic 6 times on one line.

Lines 20 and 70: This is the outer loop that causes the inner loop to be repeated 4 times. Thus the inner loop prints out a length of 6 graphics and the outer loop repeats this 4 times.

Question

1. Change Sample program 10.1 so the computer will print out a rectangle of seven graphics wide by ten graphics long.

Exercise

1. Write a program to print out the one to five times tables on the screen.

11. FLAGS

Flags in the everyday world are used to call someone's attention to something. Similarly in programming, flags signal the computer to do something.

Flags are often used in READ-DATA statements to signal the computer to stop reading the data. This way an OUT-OF-DATA error message can be avoided.

SAMPLE PROGRAM 11.1

```
10  REM USING FLAGS
20  READ A, B
30  IF A = −10000 THEN GOTO 80
40  C = A+B
50  PRINT A; "+"; B; "="; C
60  DATA 10, 2, 5, 6, 30, 34, 50, 70, 100, 200, −40, 40, 0, −3, −10000, −10000
70  GOTO 20
80  PRINT "YOU ARE NOW OUT OF DATA"
90  END
```

Questions

1. What number in the DATA line is the flag?
2. What happens when the computer reaches the flag?
3. A flag is something noticeable. How is the flag noticeable apart from the other numbers?
4. Add 10 more numbers before the flag to the DATA statement and run the program. What happens?

Flags allow the programmer to omit either a counter and an IF statement or a FOR-NEXT loop. Data can be added at any time without having to change the counter.

In the everyday world flags are highly visible. In computer programming a noticeable or "funny" number is usually chosen as a flag. Choose a number, to be used as a flag, that is unlikely to ever be used as DATA in the task for which the program is designed.

Exercise

1. Write a program that will read in a set of numbers no matter what the size and determine and print out the average. (Hint: You will need a counter in this program that will become the divisor of the sum and an adder that will sum up each number read in.)

---

12. TIME DELAY AND FLASHING SCREEN

Often, it is useful for the microcomputer to wait while the user is either reading instructions or thinking. To do this we write a time delay in the program by means of a FOR-NEXT loop. During this loop, the microcomputer is counting but not printing anything on the screen.

For example, in this loop FOR I = 1 TO 1000: NEXT I, the microcomputer is not doing anything on the screen, just counting from 1 to 1000, thus delaying the program until the microcomputer reaches 1000. If you wish to delay a longer or shorter time simply adjust the 1000 accordingly.

SAMPLE PROGRAM 12.1

```
10 REM USING A TIME DELAY
20 PRINT "THE BEGINNING"
30 PRINT "TIME DELAY"
40 FOR DELAY = 1 to 5000
50 NEXT DELAY
60 PRINT "THE END"
```

Questions

1. What happens immediately after the words TIME DELAY?
2. Approximately how long does it take for the microcomputer to count to 5000?
3. Change the time delay loop so the delay is about 10 seconds.

If you wish to have something flash on and off on the screen, you will need a time delay and a statement to clear the screen.

SAMPLE PROGRAM 12.2

```
10  PRINT "CLR"
20  PRINT "JEREMY"
30  FOR I = 1 TO 1000: NEXT I
40  GOTO 10
```

Questions

4. What would be the effect if line 40 directed the computer to go to line 20 instead of line 10?
5. What changes would be necessary to have the computer ask for the user's name and then accept the user's name and flash it on the screen?

Exercise

1. Write a simple program that flashes words in the center of the screen like a neon sign.

---

13. ON-GOTO

The ON-GOTO statement (see Figure 3.4) is used if there are several possible branches in a program. The value of the variable following the ON determines which branch is taken. For example, the line looks like this:

```
20  ON V GOTO 100, 200, 300
```

and the branching occurs like this:
if V = $-1, -2\ldots$ -----no branch taken; program continues
        0-----------no branch taken; program continues
        1-----------line 100
        2-----------line 200
        3-----------line 300
        4,5$\ldots$-----no branch taken; program continues

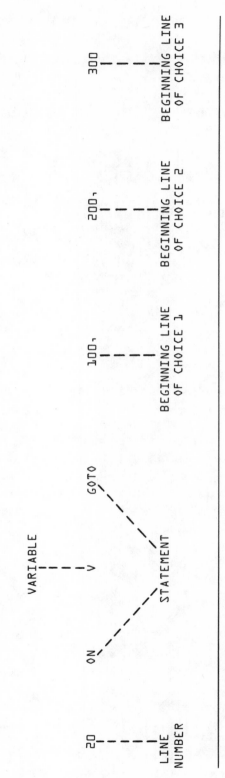

Figure 3.4: The ON-GOTO Statement

SAMPLE PROGRAM 13.1

```
10  REM THIS PROGRAM SHOWS THE USE OF THE ON-GOTO
20  PRINT "YOU HAVE THREE CHOICES FOR LUNCH"
30  PRINT "1: PIZZA"
40  PRINT "2: CHEF SALAD"
50  PRINT "3: HAMBURGER, FRENCH FRIES"
60  PRINT "CHOOSE BY NUMBER 1, 2, or 3"
70  INPUT V
80  ON V GOTO 100, 200, 300
100 PRINT "THE PIZZA HAS PEPPERONI, MUSHROOMS, AND ON-
    IONS": END
200 PRINT "CHEF SALAD IS LOWEST IN CALORIES": END
300 PRINT "YOU MUST LIKE JUNK FOOD": END
```

Questions

1. What happens if the user picks choice 2? choice 3?
2. Where does the program go if V = 1?
3. What happens if the user responds by typing a 0?
4. What happens if the user responds by typing a 4,5 . . . ?
5. Add a line to the program so that if the user picks 4,5 . . . the computer will respond "TRY AGAIN" and revert to line 20.
6. Change the program to add two more choices and print statements if these choices are selected.

ON can be also used in combination with subroutines. It then becomes ON-GOSUB (see GOSUB section).

Exercise

1. Write a "Pick a Joke" or a "Pick a Math Problem" program where the user has a choice of several options.

---

14. RANDOM NUMBERS

The RND function is one of the most useful of BASIC functions. RND is an abbreviated term for the word "random." The RND function generates random numbers. Random numbers can be either decimals or integers. The user specifies the possible upper and lower limits that the random numbers can take on. However, the range of random numbers is limited to be no smaller than −32767 and no larger than +32767. Within the range specified by the user, each number has an equal chance of being chosen.[1]

For example, think of a hat filled with balls. Each ball has a number printed on it within the specified range. All numbers within the allowed range of numbers are assigned to a ball. Pick a ball from the hat; record the number; put the ball back in the hat; stir the balls: pick another ball, and so on. The table of recorded numbers is referred to as a "random number table."

Random numbers are often used in educational programs. One frequent use is within an addition exercise, where many numerical examples are required. By using the statement RND, the numbers can be different each time, thereby making an automatic infinite problem set. Another common application is to use RND to choose various computer responses to student input, including congratulations for a correct response.

SAMPLE PROGRAM 14.1

```
10  REM THIS PROGRAM GENERATES 15 RANDOM NUMBERS
20  FOR I = 1 to 15
30  A = RND (1)
40  PRINT A
50  NEXT I
60  END
```

Questions

1. What types of numbers (integer or decimal) does this program generate?
2. Observe the numbers. Are any the same?
3. Run the program again. Compare the first set of numbers to the second. Are any the same?
4. Are the numbers greater than or less than 1?

SAMPLE PROGRAM 14.2

```
10  REM THIS PROGRAM GENERATES 15 RANDOM NUMBERS
20  FOR I = 1 TO 15
30  B = 5 * RND (1)
40  PRINT B
50  NEXT I
60  END
```

Questions

5. What type of numbers (integer or decimal) are printed?
6. How do these numbers compare to those generated after running Sample Program 14.1?
7. Change line 30 to read:
    30 B = INT (5 * RND(1))
    and run the program. What happens to the numbers?
8. What range of numbers appear to be generated? Run the program several times if necessary.
9. Change line 30 to read:
    30 B = INT (6 * RND(1))
    and run the program. What range appears this time?
10. What change should be made to line 30 to generate 0 to 6? Check your answer on the computer.
11. Change line 30 to read:
    30 B = INT (5 * RND(1) +1)
    and run the program. What range appears?
12. How is the range in question 11 different from that in question 9?
13. How could the numbers 1 to 6 be generated? Check your answer on the computer.
14. Change line 30 to read:
    30 B = INT ((5 − 2+ 1) * RND(1) + 2)
    and run the program. What range is generated?

The formulas for random integers are as follows:

FORMULA	WILL GENERATE
INT(N + 1 * RND(1))	0 TO N
INT(3 * RND(1))	0 TO 2
INT(N * RND(1) + 1)	1 TO N
INT(7 * RND(1) + 1)	1 TO 7
INT((N − M + 1) * RND(1) + M)	M TO N
INT((10 − 2 + 1) * RND(1) + 2)	2 TO 10

(Remember: The range of random integers is constrained to fall within the range −32767 to +32767.)

Questions

15. How could line 30 in Sample Program 14.2 be changed to generate the following set of integers:
    a. numbers between 0 and 100 inclusive
    b. numbers between 1 and 100 inclusive
    c. numbers between 5 and 100 inclusive
    d. numbers greater than 20 and less than 30
    e. numbers greater than or equal to 20 but less than 30

SAMPLE PROGRAM 14.3

```
10  REM THIS PROGRAM USES RANDOM NUMBERS
20  REM IN A MATHEMATICS DRILL OF THE TIMES TABLES
30  REM FROM 0 TO 12
40  FOR I = 1 TO 10
50  A = INT(13 * RND(1))
60  B = INT (13 * RND(1))
70  C = A * B
80  PRINT A; "*"; B; "=?"
90  INPUT ANS
100  IF ANS <> C GOTO 70
110  PRINT "GOOD! YOU ARE CORRECT."
120  NEXT I
130  END
```

Questions

16. How many items will be in this drill?
17. How would you change the program to drill only the 0 to 5 times tables?
18. What happens if the user continuously gets the wrong answer when using the program?
19. Change the program so the user only gets 3 chances then the correct answer is given on the screen. (Hint: A counter is needed.)
20. Change the program so the user can pick the number of items in the drill. (Hint: Use an INPUT; use a variable in the FOR-NEXT loop.)

Random numbers can also be used to select strings of random praises if a correct answer is given. Random numbers are used here in combination with the ON-GOTO statement.

SAMPLE PROGRAM 14.4

```
10  REM THIS PROGRAM RANDOMLY CHOOSES PRAISE
20  REM FOR A CORRECT ANSWER
30  X = INT(10 * RND(1) + 1): Y = INT(10 * RND(1) + 1)
40  Z = X + Y
50  PRINT X; "+"; Y; "=?"
60  INPUT ANS
70  IF ANS <> Z THEN GOTO 50
80  A = INT(5 * RND(1) + 1)
90  ON A GOTO 100, 150, 200, 250, 300
100  PRINT "GOOD"
110  END
150  PRINT "CORRECT"
160  END
200  PRINT "GOOD WORK! KEEP IT UP!"
210  END
250  PRINT "YOU GOT IT!"
260  END
300  PRINT "YOUR ANSWER IS RIGHT!"
310  END
```

Questions

21. What range of numbers is generated by lines 30 and 40?
22. What range of numbers is generated in line 80?
23. If A (line 80) becomes 3, which praise is printed?
24. How could lines 110, 160, 210, 260, and 310 be eliminated as separate lines?
25. Why may the user of Sample Program 14.4 consider it to be unnecessarily limited and frustrating to use?

Exercises

1. Write a program that generates 2 random integers between 1 and 10; the program should then randomly provide addition, subtraction, or multiplication problems that use these 2 numbers.

2. Write a guessing game program. The user must guess at a number between 1 and 25. If the guess is too small, the program prints "Your guess is too small." If the answer is too large, the program prints "Your guess is too large." If the guess is incorrect, the program returns to where the user can try another guess. If the answer is correct, the program prints "You got it!" After a correct answer, the program asks the user if he wants to play again and proceeds to the appropriate point in the program.

---

15. PEEK AND POKE

The POKE statement allows access to a position in the computer's memory so its contents can be changed. Although all of the computer's RAM memory can be accessed, the beginning programmer is probably most interested in the POKE numbers related to the video display. You should be very careful about poking into other memory locations.

The screen positions for the PET are accessed by the POKE numbers 32768 to 33767 (see Appendix D). Memory locations are numbered by row, with 32768 controlling the upper left-hand corner of the video display, to 33767 which is located at the extreme lower right-hand corner. There are 40 locations on each row (20 on the Vic 20). There are 25 rows (23 for the Vic 20). On the C64, the numbers are 1024 to 2023; on the Vic 20 the numbers are 7680 to 8185. (For information on POKE and color for the C64 and Vic 20, see your user guide that came with the computer.) The following discussion is based on the PET, except where otherwise noted.

A sample POKE statement in a program would look like this:

20	POKE	32768,	83
line #	statement	location # & comma	character #

SAMPLE PROGRAM 15.1

5 REM THIS PROGRAM SHOWS THE USE OF POKE
10 PRINT *"CLR"*
20 POKE 32768,83

(C64 - 20 POKE 1024,83)
(Vic 20 - 20 POKE 7680,83)

Question

1. What happens when this program is run?

Add this line to the program:

30 POKE 32769,83

(C64 - 30 POKE 1025,83)
(Vic 20 - 30 POKE 7681,83)

Question

2. What happens?

Add this line to the program:

40 POKE 32770,65

(C64 - 40 POKE 1026,65)
(Vic 20 - 40 POKE 7682,65)

Questions

3. What happens?
4. What is the character number for the heart?
5. What is the character number for the spade?
    (Note: The character numbers for the PET can be found in
    this book in the section "Programs for Fun." There is also a

> discussion in the PET manual, pp. 413ff., or, for the C64 and
> Vic 20, see the appendixes of the C64 or Vic 20 user's guides.)

If a character is wanted in a specific position on the screen a programmer can count numbers to that position. Often, a format sheet is used. Also, a programmer can use the following formula:

$$P = 32768 + (COL - 1) + (40 * (ROW - 1))$$

For the C64 and Vic 20, the formulas are, respectively:

$$P = 1024 + (COL - 1) + (40 * (ROW - 1))$$
$$P = 7680 + (COL - 1) + (20 * (ROW - 1))$$

Note that the formula method requires that you refer to the first row and first column as row and column 1, not row and column 0 as displayed in other books.

SAMPLE PROGRAM 15.2

```
10  REM USING THE POKE FORMULA
20  COL = 20
30  ROW = 12
40  P = 32768 + (COL - 1) + (40 * (ROW - 1))
50  POKE P,65
```

Questions

6. Where does the figure appear?
7. Approximately in what row and column does the figure appear?
8. If the figure were to appear in the 25th row and the 1st column, how would the program change?

Other POKE numbers on the PET that may be useful are:

POKE 59468,14   turns on upper- lower-case mode

POKE 59468,12   turns on upper-case graphics mode, this returns the machine to the normal operating mode

POKE 144,88   disengages the RUN-STOP button;
                      this is useful if one is prone to
                      hitting this key accidentally

POKE 144,85   reengages the RUN-STOP button

The PEEK function allows the user to "peek" into the computer's memory and see exactly what is there.

SAMPLE PROGRAM 15.3

```
5  REM THIS PROGRAM FOR THE PET GIVES THE
10  REM POKE NUMBER FOR A PARTICULAR KEY
15  REM THAT IS BEING DEPRESSED
20  PRINT PEEK(151)
30  GOTO 20
```

Questions

9. What are the character numbers for heart, diamond, spade, club?
10. What are the character numbers for : 1, 2, 3, 4, 5, 6, 7, 8, 9, 0, +, −, *, /, and RETURN?

Exercises

1. Rewrite Sample Program 15.2 to have a heart appear in the last row, middle column.

2. Write a program that will read in 4 row and 4 column positions and print a graphic character in each of the corners of the screen. It may be interesting to compare this program to Exercise 1 in the PRINT, GOTO, REM section.

3. Write a program that will divide the screen into 4 quadrants using any graphic symbol. (Hint: Use FOR-NEXT loops.)

Challenge Programs

1. Write a program that will draw 3 successively smaller rectangles on the screen.

> 2. Draw a simple happy face on the screen using graphics and the POKE statement.

16. GOSUB

A programmer may want to execute a set of statements more than once. The programmer would then use a subroutine. A subroutine is a set of program lines that may be used several times, but is included only once in the program. Each program may contain many subroutines; the subroutines are generally grouped together at the end of the large or "main program."

Each time the subroutine is accessed—or "called"—a GOSUB # # # statement is executed. The # # # is the line number where the subroutine begins.

The last line of the subroutine must contain the RETURN statement; when executed, this statement signals the computer to recommence program operations immediately following the particular GOSUB statement that branched to the subroutine (Figure 3.5). The computer will automatically remember which GOSUB was used to branch to the subroutine; therefore, the RETURN statement will always direct the computer to proceed to the correct line.

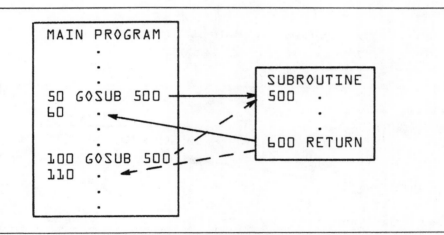

Figure 3.5: The GOSUB Statement

SAMPLE PROGRAM 16.1

```
10  REM THIS PROGRAM DETERMINES THE AVERAGE AGE,
20  REM MATH TEST SCORE, AND IQ OF
30  REM THREE STUDENTS
40  INPUT "ENTER THE AGES OF 3 STUDENTS"; X, Y, Z
50  GOSUB 500
60  PRINT "THE AVERAGE AGE IS"; AV
```

```
70  INPUT "ENTER THE IQ OF 3 STUDENTS"; X, Y, Z
80  GOSUB 500
90  PRINT "THE AVERAGE IQ IS"; AV
100 INPUT "ENTER THE MATH TEST SCORES OF 3 STUDENTS";
    X, Y, Z
110 GOSUB 500
120 PRINT "THE AVERAGE TEST SCORE IS"; AV
130 END
500 REM SUBROUTINE TO DETERMINE AVERAGES
510 AV = (X + Y + Z) / 3
520 RETURN
```

Questions

1. What line is included in the main program to call the subroutine?
2. What ending must always be at the end of the subroutine?
3. What line is included at the end of the main program to keep it from "crashing" into the subroutine?

In educational programs, subroutines are useful in giving praise for a correct answer or encouragement if the answer is incorrect (Figure 3.6).

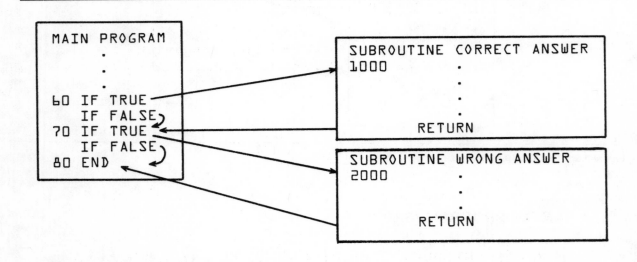

Figure 3.6: The Operation of Sample Program 16.2

SAMPLE PROGRAM 16.2

```
10  REM THIS PROGRAM SHOWS THE USE OF THE SUBROUTINE
20  REM IN PRAISING OR ENCOURAGING USERS
30  A = 5 + 4
40  PRINT "5 + 4 = ?"
50  INPUT "TYPE IN YOUR ANSWER"; ANS
60  IF ANS = A THEN GOSUB 1000
70  IF ANS <> A THEN GOSUB 2000
80  END
1000  REM SUBROUTINE TO PRAISE CORRECT ANSWER
1010  PRINT "GOOD! YOU ARE CORRECT!"
1020  RETURN
2000  REM SUBROUTINE TO NOTE AN INCORRECT ANSWER
2010  PRINT "SORRY. YOUR ANSWER IS INCORRECT."
2020  RETURN
```

Questions

4. What happens if line 60 is a true statement?
5. What happens if line 60 is not true?
6. Change the above program so that if the user gets the wrong answer the program returns to line 40 to give the user another chance. (Hint: Add another IF line at line 75.)
   (Note: A counter can be easily added to this program to give the user only a certain number of tries at this question. See Counter and Adder section.)

A good programmer regularly uses subroutines; this is referred to as "modular" or "structured" programming. The main program, after the REM and initialization statements, is generally limited to merely be a set of calls to subroutines. The main program acts as a traffic cop directing the flow of the program to the various subroutines. A modular program made up of subroutines is easier to debug. Also, once a subroutine is written, it can be used in other programs without having to rewrite it each time.

Exercises

1. Write a program that converts a Fahrenheit temperature that the user enters to Celsisus. Have the conversion formula in a subroutine, not the main program. (Formula: C = F − 32 * (5 / 9)

2. Write a program that will generate five simple random addition questions for the user, give praise for the correct answer and encouragement and a chance to try again if the answer is wrong. Give only 3 chances for the user to get the correct answer. Use subroutines. (Hint: It might be useful to review Random Numbers.)

NOTE

1. Each computer has a constant initial seed number in its permanent memory. This means that the same sequence of numbers will be generated each time the computer is turned on. To avoid this, a random seed can be generated by adding the following line near the beginning of the program before adding the first RND statement. For example, in Sample Program 14.1, add the line

15 SEED = RND(−TI)

See pages 223ff. of the PET Manual for a further discussion.

4 Educational Applications

- Educational Advantages of the Microcomputer
- Uses of the Microcomputer in the Classroom
- Administrative Uses
- Schedule and Use
- Sample Schedules

In this section, we first consider the educational advantages of the microcomputer. The various classroom applications of the microcomputer are then outlined in chart form. Finally, we present some suggestions on a reasonable distribution of microcomputers if the computer to student ratio is low in your school. Some sample timetables are also included.

EDUCATIONAL ADVANTAGES OF THE MICROCOMPUTER

We can get fellow teachers interested in using the microcomputer in the classroom by making them aware of its many advantages. These advantages accrue not only to the student but to the teacher and administration as well. These advantages include: (1) improving the skill level of the student; (2) individualizing the teacher's lessons; (3) providing instantaneous feedback; (4) increasing student motivation; (5) lessening the teacher's record-keeping burden.

First, the microcomputer is highly successful in helping develop the skills of the student. Because most students are keenly interested in the microcomputer, the attention span and concentration levels even of hyperactive students are increased when they are working with the microcomputer. Simulation games help improve both logic and reasoning skills. Students' memory skills are practiced with concentration programs. Students who write their own programs show improvement in organization. Even games, such as shooting targets or dodging missiles, can be beneficial in that they can sharpen the student's motor coordination. Students will develop an appreciation for developing typing skills; they will begin to recognize the pattern of the keys on the keyboard. The microcomputer encourages independence on the part of the user; the student is no longer a passive listener but an active participant, learning by discovery and interaction.

Secondly, the microcomputer can give as many individualized lessons as there are students. Learning is usually faster because it is at the level of the student and may even be student chosen. Students get individual attention. The microcomputer can present a varied approach to a topic and thereby reinforce concepts previously taught. It can provide remediation by means of repetition and drill. The microcomputer can present many examples; it never tires. It can provide enrichment for more advanced students. It can even help students catch up on missed work due to absenteeism.

Third, the microcomputer can provide instantaneous individual feedback to the user, thereby freeing up teacher time and indirectly helping improve the student's self-image. The student knows immediately whether the chosen answer is correct and, if necessary, can take appropriate steps to rectify his or her understanding of a given problem. The student is not faced with the embarrassment of not understanding or being wrong in front of peers.

Fourth, when microcomputers are used in the classroom, student motivation usually increases. Because of personal interaction, subjects which may have been previously boring to the students now become interesting. The student's attitude toward school or the disliked subject improves; learning is now "fun." Time on the microcomputer can become a reward. Because of the high social acceptance of the microcomputer, students feel their learning is up-to-date.

Fifth, teachers and administrators can benefit from the microcomputer's record-keeping ability. Records can be more accurate and detailed. Teachers can easily and quickly obtain student profiles. The microcomputer will free up teacher time both during class through individualized instruction and after class by performing tedious administrative chores.

USES OF THE MICROCOMPUTER
IN THE CLASSROOM

Once we are aware of the many benefits of the microcomputer in the classroom, it is up to us to use it to its fullest potential as a tool for ourselves and our students.

In the table that follows, the uses of the microcomputer are presented. The use is described along with the role of the teacher, microcomputer, and student. A short list of the advantages of a particular use is then provided.

TABLE 4.1   Uses of the Microcomputer in the Classroom

Use	Explanation	Teacher Role	Computer Role	Student Role	Advantages
CAI (computer assisted instruction)	The computer is used for presentation of instruction and possibly evaluation of how well student has grasped the material presented. Whole units may be presented. Includes drill and tutorial.	1. chooses material to be presented and adapts it as necessary 2. monitors student progress	1. presents material 2. evaluates student answers 3. branches to additional instruction if needed 4. keeps records of student progress	1. gives input as required to the computer 2. sees immediate results	1. constant teacher contact not needed 2. students proceed at self-chosen pace 3. material can be covered more quickly 4. whole units can be presented 5. results/records kept for teacher
A. Drill	The computer presents questions to student and corrects answers.	1. chooses drill and adapts it as necessary 2. monitors student progress	1. presents questions 2. corrects answers 3. keeps records of student progress	1. gives input as required to computer 2. sees immediate results	1. results to students are immediate 2. more time can be spent on drill 3. students can have as much/little practice as necessary 4. no pressure put on students for an immediate correct answer 5. easy for beginning programmer to write 6. unlimited random questions can be generated 7. results/records are kept for teacher
B. Tutorial	Instruction on one topic presented using graphics and text; quizzing of student understanding; branching to repeated or slightly varied presentation if needed	1. chooses material and adapts it as necessary 2. monitors student progress	1. presents material 2. tests and evaluates student understanding 3. branches to additional instruction as needed	1. gives input as required to computer 2. sees immediate results	1. can be used for review and reinforcement 2. is tutor for students who have been absent 3. gives additional explanation if lesson has not been understood 4. can give advanced lessons on individual basis 5. results/records are kept for teacher
Simulation	Students play major role as decision makers in hypothetical situations that simulate the real world. They are confronted with trade-offs and must evaluate and make choices.	1. gives background lessons 2. leads summarizing discussions	1. presents situation 2. computes results of student decision 3. may also play a role	1. lists and evaluates various choices 2. makes a choice 3. evaluates results of the choice	1. students are actively involved in thinking and decision-making progress 2. results of the student's decision are seen with the actual negative results being avoided
Calculator	The computer is used as a calculator to solve mathematical problems	1. selects problems 2. monitors results	1. works out mathematical calculations quickly and accurately	1. analyzes the problem 2. chooses correct formula 3. substitutes numbers into formula	1. real world problems with complicated numbers can be used 2. more problems can be done 3. active problem-solving process is emphasized; drudgery of calculations is de-emphasized 4. speed and accuracy of computer is utilized

TABLE 4.1 Continued

Use	Explanation	Teacher Role	Computer Role	Student Role	Advantages
Games	The computer is used as a presenter of animated/sound games; computer is a possible competitor and/or judge	1. sets guidelines for type of games 2. monitors results	1. plays games using displays, music 2. challenges student players 3. computes results 4. does not cheat	1. is competitor with computer, other students or himself	1. student is highly motivated 2. student must employ logical thinking skills and develop strategy 3. cheating is ruled out
Word Processor	Text is typed into computer and edited by student using word processing program that allows student to correct spelling, change words, eliminate or reposition whole phrases or paragraphs	1. assigns essay topic 2. marks rough drafts 3. evaluates final draft	1. prints student text 2. edits students text 3. prints out final copy	1. creates and types in text 2. revises text	1. secretarial skills are practiced 2. drafts are easily edited by students 3. an edited, not a first draft copy more likely to be handed in 4. students can be creative and accurate more easily 5. less tedious for students
Management	The computer is used by the teacher to manage various business aspects of the classroom.				
	a. record keeping	1. types in data (names, scores, marking formulae)	1. stores data 2. calculates marks 3. records student progress		1. calculations always accurate 2. immediate feedback 3. less record-keeping drudgery for teachers 4. indicates at a glance areas that need reinforcement
	b. word processor	1. types in text 2. revises text	1. stores text 2. edits text 3. prints out text		1. less time needed for editing 2. easier to edit
	c. generator of materials such as class lists, graphs, letters	1. types in one copy of material needed	1. stores material 2. prints out material		1. can make many accurate copies 2. saves much hand work

ADMINISTRATIVE USES

The administrative uses of the computer are similar to, but on a much larger scale than, the classroom management uses. The computer can store and accurately process large amounts of information quickly. Because of staff limitations, the computer can do tasks that would be unfeasible to do by hand.

1. *Scheduling:* The computer can timetable teacher and student class schedules, class sizes, classrooms, and extra curricular activities. (Note: A large RAM memory—48 K or greater—may be needed for these tasks. These tasks would also require a disk drive.)

2. *Attendance records:* The computer can keep accurate and timely up-to-the-minute records thus helping cut down on truancy.

3. *Office records:* The computer can store student and teacher records. Printed class and staff lists are easily obtainable and adjusted copies can be quickly processed. School finances can be processed and stored in the computer.

4. *Library records:* The computer can store book inventories, circulation lists, and overdue lists. The computer can print out reminder slips.

SCHEDULE AND USE

If you have 500 students and only 2 computers in a school, scheduling will be tight but possible. Here are several "school-tested" suggestions on the use and timetabling of the microcomputer:

1. Unless you have an elevator, divide the microcomputers according to floors. Though this may not be equitable in terms of an equal number of classes per microcomputer, it does relieve the hazards of transporting computers up and down the stairs.

2. Determine a computer area for each classroom if the microcomputer is to be transported or a central computer space/room. Divide the minutes in the day equally between classes using the microcomputer.

3. Each teacher must decide how to use the time alloted to his or her class; for example, allow the students the whole 45 minutes or divide a 45-minute alloted period into three 15-minute sessions. The teacher must also decide with what subject to use the microcomputer. (The microcomputer has more than just mathematical uses.)

4. The teacher should post a schedule. Students are responsible for knowing the time and day they are on the microcomputer, knowing the program they are to use, and getting there on time. (This also helps develop responsibility.)

5. Make sure the students are aware that they are responsible for making up any class work they miss while on the microcomputer.

6. Students must be aware of your rules regarding

a. care and operation of the microcomputer
b. eating and drinking at the microcomputer station
c. use of video games during class time
d. microcomputer etiquette including how many students at the computer at one time, relinquishing the microcomputer when the next set of users arrive
e. use of the microcomputer before and after school and during lunch
f. teacher supervision while on the microcomputer

It is a good idea to present a lesson on the use and care of the microcomputer before the students even approach the microcomputer.

SAMPLE SCHEDULES

EXAMPLE 1   Grade 7-8 school
2 computers in the school
8 classes on one floor
4 classes on another floor
Some subjects taught in homeroom, others on rotary

COMPUTER 1		COMPUTER 2		
Time Slot	Class	Time Slot	Class	
Period 1	7A	Period 1	8E	
Period 2	7B	Period 2	Science	Class times
Period 3	7C	Period 3	8F	can be
Period 4	7D	Period 4	French	shifted
Period 5	8A	Period 5	7E	according to
Period 6	8B	Period 6	7F	day of week
Period 7	8C	Period 7	Music	
Period 8	8D	Period 8	Special Education	

EXAMPLE 2   One computer per classroom

Time Slot	Use
Period 1	Subject related use
Period 2	Subject related use
Period 3	Subject related use
Period 4	As reward at teacher discretion
Lunch	Open use at teacher discretion
Period 5	Subject related use
Period 6	Subject related use
Period 7	As reward at teacher discretion

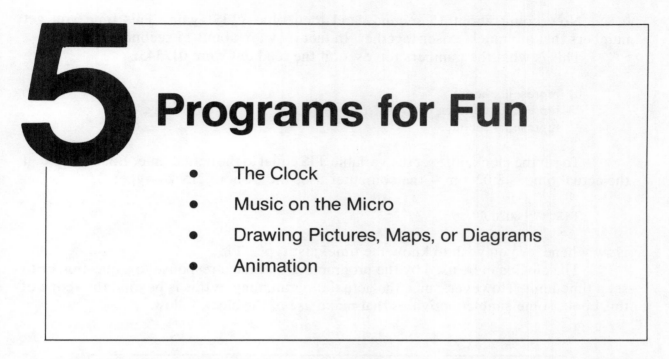

5 Programs for Fun

- The Clock
- Music on the Micro
- Drawing Pictures, Maps, or Diagrams
- Animation

In this section, several programs, ostensibly for pure enjoyment, are described and listed. While they are fun to do, they also provide practice in using various statements, such as FOR-NEXT and POKE, using the cursor, and computer logic. All these programs can be easily rewritten to conform to your own unique requirements or preferences.

These programs include clock, a utility that keeps track of the time and shows the internal clock of the computer; music, a program that directs the user in a stepwise manner to write songs that utilize the microcomputer speakers; art, a guide to using computer graphics in combination with POKE numbers; and animation, a program that moves graphics across and up and down the screen.

THE CLOCK

Every computer has a clock inside it that is turned on when the computer is turned on. The following line will show the beginning user the clock in action.

1. Type: ?TI and press RETURN

Try this again in a few seconds. What did you see happen on the screen each time?

Did you notice the first number is smaller than the second number? The clock is counting and you have printed out the length of time that the machine has been turned on. The time unit being used is called a "jiffy," 1/60 of a second.

2. Type: ?TI$ and press RETURN

Now count about 15 seconds and then type ?TI$ again. This time you get numbers that are much closer together. In fact they are about 15 seconds apart.

This is what the numbers represent if the read out were 012345:

01 represents hours
23 represents minutes
45 represents seconds

To set the clock, just set the variable TI$ equal to the actual time. For example, if the actual time is 8:02 a.m.—the computer uses the 24-hour clock—type:

TI$ = "080200"

Now whenever you wish to know the time, just type ?TI$.

The clock can be used by the programmer to time a response to a question or to set a time limit. However, since the actual programming of this is beyond the scope of this book, some simpler activities that make use of the clock follow.

Suggested Activities

1. Write a short program that will continually print out the time. (Hint: Use a loop.)

2. Write programs that will print the time in various locations on the screen, for example, center, upper right corner, upper left corner, and so on.

MUSIC ON THE MICRO

Newer PETs, the C64, and Vic 20 have a built-in speaker(s) and can generate music so that you can add sound to enhance your programs. This section will discuss music on the PET. The PET is the simplest to understand, and, therefore, perhaps the best for a beginner to start with. It is unfortunate for the beginner that the PET is different from the C64 which is different from the Vic 20 in both programming steps and note values. Consulting the user's manual for the C64 and Vic 20 will help you expand on the simple music programs contained here.

In this section, we begin with a program that plays one note. An explanation of how it works follows. Then the program is altered so a melody is played. Finally, a table giving the value of certain notes is presented.

```
10  POKE 59467,16: REM TURNS SOUND ON
20  POKE 59466,15: REM SETS OCTAVE (CHOOSE 15, 51, OR 85)
50  POKE 59464,237: REM SETS FREQUENCY (MIDDLE C)
60  T = TI: REM START THE DURATION OF THE NOTE
70  IF TI − T < 20 THEN 70: REM PLAY NOTE FOR 20 JIFFIES (1/3 SEC)
80  POKE 59467,0: REM TURN SOUND OFF
100 END
```

Run this program and you will hear middle C played for 1/3 second. Changing 237 in line 50 to another value will generate different notes. These are listed in the table of notes at the end of this section.

Note that no matter which Commodore computer you use, the sound (volume) must be turned on or set, notes and their duration chosen, and the sound (volume) turned off at the end. The POKE numbers and note values are, however, different. With the C64 and Vic 20, there are also additional steps, such as choosing the speakers to be used, setting the waveform, choosing attack/decay levels, and so on.

Now let's play a melody. To do this you will need to read in some notes and durations for each one. First you will need a variable in place of the 237 in line 50. Try N for note. Line 50 should now read:

```
50  POKE 59464,N: REM PLAY THE NOTES
```

The value of N will have to be read in, so add line 30:

```
30  READ N
```

Second, you will need a variable in place of 20 in line 70. Try D for duration. Line 70 should now read:

```
70  IF TI − T < D THEN 70: REM PLAYS NOTE FOR VARYING DURA-
TION
```

The duration will also have to be read in, so change line 30 to read:

```
30  READ N, D
```

TI is the variable for the clock that is built into the PET. This clock starts to count as soon as the microcomputer is turned on. It counts in 1/60 of second. Each 1/60 of a second is called a jiffy. (See section on the PET clock.) Line 60 sets a variable T equal to TI. TI continues to count but T is used to remember what TI was when it was set. Line 70 checks to see if the difference between these two values is 20 or 1/3 of a second and if it is not, then the microcomputer goes back to line 70 to check until the difference is 20 before going on to the next line.

In this program, you will need to stop the sequence of notes being read in. You can do this by setting one note equal to 0 in the data. Then you tell the microcomputer to stop if it reads this value. To do this, add the following line:

40 IF N = 0 THEN 90

The DATA statement will contain the scale played in 1/6 of a second for each note. You can change these if you wish.

Line 90 turns the sound off. You can use this POKE number if the sound happens to stay on for some reason.

Finally, you will need to have the microcomputer go back and continue to read each note and duration. To do this, add the following line:

80 GOTO 30

In the DATA statement, the data come in pairs. The first number is the note number; the second number is the duration number. The DATA statement is as follows:

110 DATA 237, 10, 211, 10, 188, 10, 177, 10, 157, 10, 140, 10, 124, 10, 117, 10, 0, 0

Your final program should look like this:

```
 10  POKE 59467,16
 20  POKE 59466,15
 30  READ N, D
 40  IF N = 0 THEN 90
 50  POKE 59464,N
 60  T = TI
 70  IF TI − T < D THEN 70
 80  GOTO 30
 90  POKE 59467,0
100  END
110  DATA 237, 10, 211, 10, 188, 10, 177, 10, 157, 10, 140, 10, 124, 10, 117, 10, 0, 0
```

Table of Notes

Octave	B	C	C#	D	D#	E	F	F#	G	G#	A	A#
Higher	251	237	224	211	199	188	177	167	157	149	140	132
Lower	124	117	111	104	99	93	88	83	78	73	69	

DRAWING PICTURES, MAPS, OR DIAGRAMS

The following program allows the user to practice POKE numbers and the READ-DATA statement. While a geographical diagram is presented here, the basic program can be used with different POKE numbers to create the user's own drawing, map, or diagram on the screen.

To proceed with a graphic display, a rough sketch of the picture should first be drawn on a screen format sheet (see Appendix D) or graph paper. The total number of symbols used should be counted and this number placed in line 50 of the program.

The particular POKE number of each graphic on the PET can be found in the chart in Figure 5.1. To use the chart, choose the appropriate column in the chart, either NORMAL or REVERSE mode, for a particular graphic. Add the column number of the graphic to the row number of that graphic. This gives you the POKE number for the chosen graphic. For example, the column number of the heart graphic in NORMAL mode is 80 and the row number is 3; therefore, the POKE number for the heart is 80 + 3 or 83.

Most of the POKE numbers for the graphic characters are the same on the C64 and Vic 20. However, there are some differences; check your user's guide for a complete listing. If you are using a C64 or Vic 20, POKE number 28 showing the rain in the diagram (appearing 11 times in lines 230-250 and 4 times in lines 450-460) should be changed to 77 or some other appropriate character.

DRAWING PROGRAM

```
10  REM THIS PROGRAM DRAWS A GEOGRAPHY DIAGRAM
20  REM USING POKE NUMBERS AND READ-DATA STATEMENTS
30  REM N IS THE NUMBER OF TIMES A GRAPHIC IS USED
40  PRINT "CLR"
50  N = 145
60  FOR I = 1 TO N
70  READ ROW, COL, SYMBOL
80  P = 32768 + (COL−1) + (40 * (ROW −1))
90  POKE P,SYMBOL
100  NEXT I
```

	REVERSE MODE 128	138	148	158	168	178	188	198	208	218	228	238	248
	NORMAL MODE 0	10	20	30	40	50	60	70	80	90	100	110	120
0	@	J	T	↑	(	2	<	▤	▢	◆	▢	▢	▢
1	A	K	U	←	)	3	=	▥	●	⊞	▢	▢	▢
2	B	L	V	SPACE	*	4	>	▯	▢	◧	■	▢	▢
3	C	M	W	!	+	5	?	▢	♥	▯	▢	▢	▢
4	D	N	X	"	,	6		▢	▢	▯	π	▢	▢
5	E	O	Y	#	-	7	♠	▢	▢	◣	◣	⊞	▢
6	F	P	Z	$	·	8		▯	▢	⊠	SPACE	▢	▢
7	G	Q	[	%	/	9		▢	◺	○	◨	▢	■
8	H	R	\	&	0	:		▢	◿	♣	▢	▢	▢
9	I	S	]	`		;		▢	▢	▢	▢	▢	▢

Figure 5.1: Character POKE Numbers

```
110 REM LINE 120 KEEPS CURSOR AND READY FROM APPEAR-
ING ON SCREEN
120 GET A$: IF A$ = " " THEN 120
130 END
140 REM TITLE OF DIAGRAM
150 DATA 3, 3, 20, 3, 4, 8, 3, 5, 5, 3, 7, 18, 3, 8, 1, 3, 9, 9, 3, 10, 14, 3, 12, 2, 3, 13, 1
160 DATA 3, 14, 18, 3, 15, 18, 3, 16, 9, 3, 17, 5, 3, 18, 18, 3, 20, 5, 3, 21, 6, 3, 22, 6
170 DATA 3, 23, 5, 3, 24, 3, 3, 25, 20, 3, 27, 15, 3, 28, 6, 3, 30, 13, 3, 31, 15, 3, 32, 21
180 DATA 3, 33, 14, 3, 34, 20, 3, 35, 1, 3, 36, 9, 3, 37, 14, 3, 38, 19
190 REM CLOUDS AND RAIN
200 DATA 6, 17, 85, 6, 18, 73, 6, 19, 73, 6, 20, 73, 6, 21, 85, 6, 22, 73
```

```
210  DATA 7, 17, 40, 7, 20, 85, 7, 21, 73, 7, 22, 41, 7, 23, 41, 8, 17, 74
220  DATA 8, 18, 73, 8, 19, 85, 8, 20, 75, 8, 21, 74, 8, 22, 73, 8, 23, 75
230  DATA 9, 18, 74, 9, 19, 74, 9, 21, 85, 9, 22, 75, 9, 23, 75, 10, 20, 28
240  DATA 10, 21, 28, 10, 22, 28, 11, 20, 28, 11, 21, 28, 11, 22, 28
250  DATA 12, 20, 28, 12, 21, 28, 12, 23, 28, 13, 23, 28, 14, 22, 28
260  REM MOUNTAIN
270  DATA 9, 16, 78, 9, 17, 77, 10, 15, 78, 10, 18, 77, 11, 14, 78, 11, 18, 103
280  DATA 12, 14, 101, 12, 18, 103, 13, 14, 101, 13, 19, 77
290  DATA 14, 13, 78, 14, 19, 103, 15, 12, 78, 15, 20, 77, 16, 12, 101
300  DATA 16, 21, 77, 17, 11, 78, 17, 22, 101, 18, 10, 78, 18, 22, 77
310  DATA 19, 9, 78, 19, 23, 77, 20, 8, 78, 20, 24, 77, 21, 7, 78, 21, 26, 101
320  DATA 21, 25, 99, 22, 6, 78, 22, 26, 77, 23, 2, 99, 23, 3, 99
330  DATA 23, 4, 99, 23, 5, 99, 23, 26, 103, 24, 27, 77
340  REM SEA
350  DATA 23, 27, 120, 23, 28, 120, 23, 29, 120, 23, 30, 120, 23, 31, 120
360  DATA 23, 32, 120, 23, 33, 120, 23, 34, 120
370  REM DESERT
380  DATA 22, 2, 88, 22, 4, 88
390  REM FOREST
400  DATA 18, 23, 65, 19, 24, 65, 20, 25, 65
410  REM LEGEND
420  DATA 10, 30, 88, 10, 31, 88, 10, 32, 88, 10, 34, 4, 10, 35, 5, 10, 36, 19, 10, 37, 5
430  DATA 10, 38, 18, 10, 39, 20, 12, 30, 65, 12, 31, 65, 12, 32, 65
440  DATA 14, 30, 120, 14, 31, 120, 14, 32, 120, 14, 34, 19, 14, 35, 5, 14, 36, 1
450  DATA 16, 30, 28, 16, 31, 28, 16, 34, 18, 16, 35, 1, 16, 36, 9, 16, 37, 14
460  DATA 17, 30, 28, 17, 31, 28, 12, 34, 6, 12, 35, 15, 12, 36, 18
470  DATA 12, 37, 5, 12, 38, 19, 12, 39, 20
```

Suggested Activity

1. Write a program that will "draw" a map including a legend on the screen.

ANIMATION

An interesting and most useful function of the microcomputer is its ability to simulate movement. Movement or animation is often incorporated in educational software to increase student motivation and interest.

In the first Challenge Program in the PEEK and POKE section of BASIC programming, a graphic character was moved in a rectangular path around the screen.

POKE statements were used for the placement of the figure in the various screen positions. However, graphic characters can also be moved about the screen using cursor control and FOR-NEXT loops. The following section will show you how to make a "shooting star" move in various directions over the screen using cursor control.

The cursor indicates the position on the screen where the next character typed will be located. The cursor then moves to the next position after a character has been printed.

Type: PET

Note that the cursor is now after the T. If you move back to the E by using the cursor control buttons, you will note that nothing has been erased and that the cursor is flashing over the E. Now if you press the space bar, the E will be erased and the cursor is now flashing over the next column where the T is.

If we print a character, move the cursor back over the character, then erase it using the space bar (the cursor is now in the next column after the space); print the character again, move the cursor back over this second character and erase it; then repeat this process over and over, we have simulated movement in our program. This same basic process can be used no matter in which direction—right, left, up, down—or combination of directions—diagonal—we are moving.

In the following program, using cursor control, a "star" appears to move or shoot around the screen. Detailed REM statements, which can be left out when you type in the program, should help you follow the sequence of steps.

Symbols used in the program are the following:

* - an asterisk used for the star
__ - space bar
↑ - cursor up
↓ - cursor down
→ - cursor right
← - cursor left

ANIMATION PROGRAM

```
5  REM MOVING A STAR AROUND THE SCREEN
10  PRINT "CLR": REM CLEAR THE SCREEN
20  PRINT "*";: REM PRINT * OR OTHER GRAPHIC, KEEP CURSOR
ON SAME LINE
30  FOR C = 1 TO 39: REM REPEAT FOLLOWING PROCEDURE 39
TIMES
```

```
40  PRINT "←_*";: REM MOVE CURSOR BACK, PRINT SPACE TO
ERASE *, PRINT * AGAIN
45  FOR T = 1 TO 50: NEXT T: REM TIMING LINE TO SLOW PROCE-
DURE
50  NEXT C
55  REM AT THIS POINT WE ARE IN RIGHTMOST COLUMN OF
FIRST ROW
60  FOR D = 1 TO 25: REM DO FOLLOWING 25 TIMES
70  PRINT "←_ ↓ ←*";: REM MOVE CURSOR BACK, PRINT SPACE
TO ERASE *. GO DOWN AND BACK AND PRINT * AGAIN.
75  FOR T = 1 TO 50: NEXT T: REM TIMING LINE
80  NEXT D
85  REM NOW WE ARE IN BOTTOM RIGHT CORNER OF SCREEN
90  FOR X = 1 TO 39: REM DO FOLLOWING 39 TIMES
100  PRINT "←_← ←*";: REM MOVE CURSOR BACK, PRINT A
SPACE TO ERASE *. MOVE CURSOR BACK TWICE AND PRINT *
AGAIN.
105  FOR T = 1 TO 50: NEXT T: REM TIMING LINE
110  NEXT X
115  REM WE ARE NOW IN LOWER LEFT CORNER
120  FOR Y = 1 TO 25: REM DO FOLLOWING 25 TIMES
130  PRINT "←_ ↑ ←*";: REM MOVE CURSOR BACK, PRINT SPACE
TO ERASE THE *. GO UP AND BACK AND PRINT * AGAIN.
135  FOR T = 1 TO 50: NEXT T: REM TIMING LINE
140  NEXT Y
150  END
```

Movement does not have to begin at the home position. You can start your graphic character in any screen position by printing it there using a PRINT statement with cursor control or by POKEing the character into a particular position.

Movement, also, does not have to be strictly right, left, up, or down. By combining up-down motion with right-left motion, diagonal movement can be simulated.

Suggested Activities

1. Write a program that will incorporate diagonal movement in it.

2. Write a program with a "ball" graphic character, in which the ball bounces up and down across the screen.

3. Using appropriate characters, have a comet circling a sun (or a planet moving around a sun).

4. Simulate the 9 planets of our solar system moving around the sun.

6 Getting the Most from the Microcomputer

- Troubleshooter's Guide
- Features of Good Educational Software
- Teacher Involvement with Microcomputers
- System Commands
- PET Personality

This chapter is divided into five sections. The first section serves as a guide to teachers and students, and can be posted at the microcomputer station, on how to recover from a failure on the part of the microcomputer system or software. The second section lists features you may want to consider when buying software for your microcomputer. The third section gives some suggestions on how to get other teachers interested in the microcomputer as a valuable classroom tool. A quick reference to the Commodore system commands is provided in the fourth section; this could also be posted at the microcomputer station. Section five can also serve as a handy reference and gives a list of "personality quirks" of the PET, most of which also apply to the Commodore 64 and the Vic 20 as noted.

TROUBLESHOOTER'S GUIDE

It is inevitable that students will encounter problems when working with the microcomputer either because the software they are working with is not "bullet proof" or because they are not yet experienced or confident enough to tackle these problems. It will be very inconvenient if you must stop your lesson each time the student users encounter a problem; it will be still worse if you can't determine quickly what's wrong or how to get the students back into the program.

Below is a list of "snags" you or your students may encounter and how to solve them quickly. We recommend that a list of these be posted at your microcomputer station so student users are able to cope themselves.

Snag 1

PROBLEM: The computer doesn't turn on or blanks out in the middle of a program.

REASON: Probably electrical.

SOLUTION: Check that the plug and/or extension cords are firmly plugged in. Check that the cord and cassette recorder are firmly plugged into the microcomputer jacks on the back of the microcomputer. Retighten each connection by hand.

(Note: Do *not* plug the cassette recorder in if the microcomputer is on.)

Snag 2

PROBLEM: The program stops in the middle and the screen says READY.

REASON: You have "dropped out" of your program perhaps because you didn't give the microcomputer a type of answer it required.

SOLUTION: Type CONT for the program to resume again where it left off or type RUN and begin the program again.

Snag 3

PROBLEM: During or after loading, the screen says LOAD ERROR.

REASON: Parts of the tape haven't loaded correctly, *or* tape heads are either out of alignment or dirty.

SOLUTION: Rewind the tape and try to load again. Use one of the many commercial products to clean the tape heads.

(Note: There may be some permanent damage to your tape or the program on your tape is not compatible with your type of microcomputer. In either case, your tape will simply not load. However, if you are sure the tape is all right and you get LOAD ERROR the second time, it may take 3 to 5 times before it will load correctly. Keep trying and be patient. A good idea is to load the tape once and have each set of student users rerun the program without turning off the machine each time. If tape heads are out of alignment, a trained person will have to fix it.)

Snag 4

PROBLEM: In running the program, you encounter SYNTAX ERROR LINE #.

REASON: (a) The program was not written correctly.

(b) The program was not loaded into the microcomputer correctly.

SOLUTION: (a) You must debug the program yourself or you cannot use the program.

(b) Type NEW to clear the microcomputer's memory and reload the program.

Snag 5

PROBLEM: In the middle of the program, you encounter REDO FROM START.

REASON: You have either given an incorrect type of answer or no answer.

SOLUTION: Type in the correct type of answer and the program will proceed.

Snag 6

PROBLEM: The microcomputer "crashes," that is, nothing happens no matter which keys you hit.

REASON: Various electronic reasons, for example, dirty connectors or the program is not designed to run on your type of microcomputer.

SOLUTION: Try pressing RETURN several times. Then try to break out of the program by pressing RUN-STOP. If neither works, you can even consider using the "Mash Method": gently press down many keys with the palm of your hand; remarkably, if you are using a commercial assembly language program, this may be the only solution. If nothing else works turn off the computer, turn it back on, and start all over.

Snag 7

PROBLEM: The program requires a response from the user, but you don't know what to type in.

REASON: Often the instructions are poorly written or not given, so the user must guess how to proceed.

SOLUTION: Look at what is last on the screen. Does there seem to be a choice? If so, type in a number or letter indicating your choice. If there seems to be no choice indicated, try several numbers to see if the program will proceed.

FEATURES OF GOOD EDUCATIONAL SOFTWARE

There is an abundance of software on the market today that is of low quality and questionable educational value. This checklist presents features you might consider when evaluating software for use in your classroom or school. It is unlikely that any one program will contain all of these features; this checklist is meant to serve as a guideline for your particular requirements.

PEDAGOGY

1. The program is correct in content and performance.
2. Provision for varying degrees of skill is made.
3. The timing seems appropriate: the program is not too long to be boring nor incapable of being completed in the alloted time.

4. The material presented is appropriate to the computer:
   a. Must the student use a pencil and paper?
   b. Can the same lesson be done with a textbook?
5. Not too much material is presented at once.
6. The program is well documented:
   a. There are REMark statements to help in understanding how the program works.
   b. Variables are explained through remarks or in a teacher's manual.
   c. There is a teacher's manual.
   d. There are student worksheets.

OBJECTIVES

1. The objectives of the program are stated.
2. The objectives are clear.
3. The program follows its stated objectives.

INSTRUCTIONS

1. Instructions are provided for the user.
2. Instructions are clear and concise.
3. Instructions are at the level of the student users and there is not too much to remember.
4. Instructions are an optional feature.
5. Instructions can be retrieved by the user during the program run.
6. Clear, concise examples are included in the instructions.
7. Instructions that occur more than once are consistent in their language.

USER FRIENDLY AND BULLET PROOF

1. The user does not drop out of the program when RETURN alone (without an accompanying answer) is pressed.
2. The user does not drop out of the program when the RUN-STOP key is pressed.
3. The user does not drop out of the program if any wrong key is pressed.
4. The program accepts and uses the name of the user.
5. The user gets more than one chance to answer a question.
6. The user can continue with the program if unsuccessful in answering a question.
7. The program is user paced.
8. Feedback at the end of each question and at the end of the program is provided.
9. There is positive rather than negative feedback.
10. The user can obtain *help* if needed during the program.
11. The program loads easily.

CONTENT

In addition to the software being "user friendly," we as teachers must take appropriate measures to insure that all information presented to students is both accurate and sensitive to social norms. This is particularly true when material is presented via a microcomputer since by its nature as an instructional medium the personal element of the teacher is eliminated.

Students may be aware that teachers and books are not infallible; however, the judgment of the student may be less critical when the same information is presented from microcomputers. There is a general belief that what eminates from the computer is truth; time and familiarity with computers will change this. However, for these reasons, it is extremely important that the content of microcomputer software be thoroughly evaluated before its purchase or use; this is particularly true when selecting games.

The following is a partial list of criteria that can be used when selecting software for educational use:

1. The software should exhibit neither racism nor sexism.
2. Reject programs that are based upon simplified occupational, ethnic, cultural, and national/regional stereotypes.
3. Animals and their behavior should not be misrepresented. For example, gorillas are often represented as aggressive, vicious killers; in fact, gorillas are relatively shy.
4. Animals should not be portrayed in a demeaning manner. Animals should not be portrayed as being exploited by people. Animals should not be the object of conflict and destroy games.

ORGANIZATION AND COSMETICS

1. Only one idea, concept, or type of problem is presented on the screen at a time.
2. The information on the screen is well spaced; the screen is not cluttered.
3. Any words broken up on the screen are broken correctly between syllables.
4. Spelling and grammar are correct.
5. Questions where possible are randomly generated.
6. If any keys are disabled, for example the RUN-STOP, they are enabled at the end of the program.
7. Sounds, if used, are not distracting to others.

RECORD-KEEPING OPTIONS

(Some programs have record-keeping options. If so, here are some features to consider.)

1. Record keeping is a teacher option.
2. Record keeping is accurate.
3. A record of the number of tries at an answer is kept for the teacher.
4. If the user ends the program, the records are maintained.
5. Records can only be accessed by the teacher or by a student accessing his or her own personal records.

TEACHER INVOLVEMENT WITH MICROCOMPUTERS

Many teachers may be distressed about the advent of microcomputers in the classroom. Some teachers may imagine their authority being undermined by students who are more knowledgeable about microcomputers; others may consider the microcomputer a threat to their job security—a future replacement of themselves. This fear must be eliminated if we are to successfully use the computer in the classroom.

How do we eliminate fear of the microcomputer? Answer: The teacher must be involved with the microcomputer in the classroom. We suggest that you may use the following courses of action to get teachers to embrace the current technology:

1. Start by working together with a small group of other interested teachers.
2. Get an administrator interested—your principal if possible.
3. Put a microcomputer in a classroom of one of the interested teachers. Help the teacher and students in this classroom to use the microcomputer.
4. Get together every few days in the classroom with the teachers who have the microcomputers to iron out any difficulties. Make these sessions short, no more than twenty minutes.
5. Students are exceedingly enthusiastic about microcomputers; remember, this is the age of the computer game. So, transfer this interest to educational programs. Do this as soon as possible so that the computer is viewed by the students and the other teachers as more than a toy.
6. Form a microcomputer club. It is most important at the beginning to get students that are enthusiastic; don't just emphasize the mere number of student members.
7. Don't overwhelm beginners with computer technology and terminology. Make the computer seem simple and understandable.
8. Prepare a one-page set of instructions on the operation of the microcomputer that can be used by students and teachers as a handy reference. Post one copy by the microcomputer.
9. Inform teachers about available software that relates to their areas of interest. Let them know what this software does. Include information about how they can obtain this software. However, initially, you should actually provide it for them; they will not yet be motivated enough to seek it out themselves.

10. Help teachers set up a time schedule for the use of the microcomputer by their students.

11. Hold workshops for the teachers in your school, showing them how to use the microcomputer and its value in the classroom.

12. Establish a software collection in your school with programs in various subject areas.

13. Provide up-to-date reference materials on the educational applications of the microcomputer.

14. If teachers don't want microcomputers in their classroom at this time, volunteer your class area as a central computer area to which their students can be sent.

15. Volunteer to work out the problems students might have when they come to your area to work on the microcomputer.

16. Try to get microcomputer workshops as an activity on professional development days.

17. Have student presentations on the microcomputer on parents' nights.

18. Provide teachers with information on microcomputer workshops and courses for beginners offered nearby.

19. Get the support of the school board. Present to them hands-on workshops that stress the value of the microcomputer to education. Without the board's monetary support there will be no microcomputers in education.

20. Volunteer to teach microcomputer workshops to other teachers in your school board.

21. Reward involved teachers with support and praise. Try to get them release time and monetary reimbursement for microcomputer workshops.

22. Go to workshops and conferences yourself to keep abreast of the newest information and innovations that can be taken back to your school.

23. Be enthusiastic. Always stress the positive aspects of the microcomputer. Be a propagandist for it as a valuable educational tool wherever and whenever possible.

SYSTEM COMMANDS

If you wish to:

1. LOAD a program from tape

       Put cassette in tape drive
       Rewind tape
       Type: LOAD
       Press: RETURN
       The computer will give you instructions on the screen

(Note: This will load the first program on the tape that the computer finds.)

2. LOAD a specific program from tape

    Rewind tape
    Type: LOAD "name of program"
    Press: RETURN
    The computer will give you instructions on the screen

3. RUN a program after it has been loaded

    Type: RUN
    Press: RETURN

4. STOP the computer in the middle of a program or listing

    Press: RUN-STOP key

5. CLEAR a program from the memory

    Type: NEW
    Press: RETURN

6. LIST the set of instructions of the program

    Type: LIST
    Press: RETURN

7. SAVE a program onto a tape

    Insert blank tape into cassette drive
    Rewind tape
    Type: SAVE "name of program"
    Press: RETURN
    The computer will give you instructions on the screen

8. VERIFY program

    Rewind tape
    Type: VERIFY
    Press: RETURN
    The computer will give you instructions on the screen

9. CORRECT an error

    a. Before you've pressed RETURN:
       Press the INST-DEL key as often as necessary to go back to the error.
       Retype your text
    b. After you've pressed RETURN:
       Move cursor to letter (s) to be changed.
       Retype as needed

10. CONTINUE when you drop out of a program

    Type: CONT
    Press: RETURN
    The computer will return to the point where you dropped out of the program

PET PERSONALITY

(Those marked with an * apply also to the C64 and Vic 20.)

*A. SYSTEM COMMANDS

1. LOAD or LOAD "name"
    Loads a program from cassette to computer.
2. RUN
    Causes the execution of the program in memory.
3a. LIST
    Lists entire program from beginning.
  b. LIST 100
    Lists only line 100.
  c. LIST 100-
    Lists the program beginning at line 100.
  d. LIST 100-200
    Lists lines 100 to 200 inclusive.
  e. LIST -100
    Lists lines to line 100.
4a. SAVE
    Saves a program in memory onto tape.
  b. SAVE "name"
    Saves program called "name" onto tape.
5. NEW
    Clears the memory of any program. (Note: You can also turn off the computer to
    clear the memory.)

6.   Abbreviations
     Each of the above except for NEW can be abbreviated using the first letter and the
     second letter shifted.

B. USEFUL POKE NUMBERS

1. Upper and lower case

    POKE 59468,14

2. Graphics and upper case

    POKE 59468,12

    (This is the mode when the machine is turned on.)

3. Putting a character on the screen

    POKE 32768 to 33767, # #

    Example: POKE 32768 is the location of the home position on the screen.
    Therefore, POKE 32768,83 pokes a heart onto that location on the screen. Other
    numbers for the characters can be found in the Fun Programs chapter.

4. Determining exact location on the screen
    Use the following formula:

    $P = 32768 + (COL - 1) + (40 * (ROW -))$

    Example: The POKE number for the fifteenth position over and the twentieth
    position down would be

    $P = 32768 + (15 - 1) + (40* (20-1))$
    $= 32768 + 14 + 760$
    $= 33542$

5. Making music

a.	POKE 59467,16	Turns sound on.
b.	POKE 59467,0	Turns sound off.
c.	POKE 59464, # # #	Plays the note.
d.	POKE 59464,0	Turns note off.
e.	POKE 59466,15	Picks the octave to be 15, from the choice of 15, 51, or 85.

6. To disable the RUN-STOP key

    POKE 144,88

7. To enable the RUN-STOP key

    POKE 144,85

*C. CALCULATOR MODE

1. To perform calculations
    Use ? then the problem.
    Example:

    ?2 + 3

2. Order of operations

    a. brackets   ( )
    b. exponents   ↑
    c. unary minus   −
    d. multiplication or   *
        division   /
    e. addition or   +
        subtraction   −

3. Relational operators

    = equal to
    < less than
    > greater than
    <> not equal to
    >= greater than or equal to
    <= less than or equal to

4. Scientific notation
    Used when results are over 8 digits long.
    Example:

    $243678789 = 2.43679E + 08$
    $.0000000001 = 1E - 10$

5. Accuracy
   8 to 9 significant digits.
6. Largest number

   1.70141183E + 38

   Smallest number

   2.93873588E − 39

*D. STATEMENT NOTES

1. REM
   Remark statement used by programmer to document program.
   Ignored by the computer.
2. PRINT
   "Shorthand" form is ?
3. LET
   Use is optional.
   LET X = 5 is the same as X = 5.
4. IF-THEN
   Statements after THEN only executed when IF part is true.
   Example:

   IF X = 6 THEN PRINT D

   D is only printed if X = 6.
5. GET
   Used to input one character.
   Example:

   ```
   10  GET S$
   20  IF S$ = " " THEN 10
   30  PRINT S$
   ```

6. CONT
   To restart program where user left off.

7. VERIFY
   Checks if program on screen was properly stored to cassette or disk.

E. PROGRAMMING NOTES

1. Program lines
   May be up to 2 display lines long or 80 characters.
*2. : (colon)
   Can be used to write multiple statements on one display line.
   Example:

   10 FOR X = 1 TO 10: PRINT D: NEXT X

*3. Strings
   Maximum 255 characters long including spaces.
*4. Cursor movement
   Can be programmed into PRINT statements using quotes.
   Example:

   10 PRINT "→ → → DOG"

   Will print DOG 3 spaces to the right of the margin.
*5. Clear screen during program run
   Use PRINT statement and press CLR HOME placing it between quotation marks.
*6. , (comma)
   Divides screen into 4 fields of 10 characters each.
*7. Variables
   May be names using 1, 2, or 3 characters.
   Use unshifted letter for first character of variable name.
   If using 3, the last one must either be a $ for a string or a % for an integer.
   Certain two-letter combinations not allowed; therefore, avoid two-letter variable names.
   Those not allowed: LE, TI, ST, ON, IF

*F. CLOCK

The microcomputer has a built-in clock that starts at 000000 when turned on. To set the time, type TI$ = "124550" where 12 is an example of the hour. 45 is an example of the minutes, and 50 is an example of the seconds. To read the time, type ?TI$ whenever the computer says READY. It is best to set the time ahead by a minute or two and press RETURN at exactly the correct time.

APPENDIX A

SOLUTIONS TO CHAPTER 3

PRINT, GOTO, AND REM ANSWERS

QUESTIONS

1a. WHAT IS YOUR NAME?
 b. 10 PRINT "   "
2. It signals the end of the program to the computer. This statement is not needed, but it is good practice to include it. For the time being, END statements will be left out; as programs become more complex, an END statement will be included.
3. A rocket.
4. The rocket moves up the screen (called scrolling) over and over.
5. Prints a space; it is like a carriage return on a typewriter.
6. Quotation marks.
7. No.
8. Comma spaces across the screen. Semicolon eliminates spaces between words.
9. Insert a space after the word HI or before the word HOW; the space should be inside the quotation marks.
10. It spaces from the left margin.
11. A means to insert remarks about what is happening in the program or a particular line.
12. It clears the screen.
13. Letters themselves are black on the PET.
14. Green on the PET.
15. Keeps branching to line 30. (It is used to keep READY and the cursor from flashing on the screen at the end of your program. It can be stopped by pressing the RUN-STOP key.)

EXERCISES

1.
```
10 REM DRAWING A HEART NEAR EACH CORNER
20 PRINT "CLR"
30 PRINT " ♥ ";TAB(39);" ♥ "
40 PRINT "↓↓↓↓↓↓↓↓↓↓↓↓↓↓↓↓↓↓↓↓ ♥ ";TAB(39);"♥ "
50 GOTO 50
```

2.
```
10 REM WRITING YOUR NAME NEAR THE CORNERS
20 PRINT"CLR"
30 PRINT "SUE"; TAB(30); "SUE"
40 PRINT"↓↓↓↓↓↓↓↓↓↓↓↓↓↓↓↓↓↓↓↓↓↓↓↓↓SUE";  TAB(30);
"SUE"
50 GOTO 50
```

3. Same as 2 above except add these lines:

```
45 PRINT "HOME" (means home-the-cursor button)
46 PRINT "↓↓↓↓↓↓↓↓↓↓↓↓"; TAB(15); "R SUE"
```

VARIABLES: LET STATEMENT ANSWERS

Questions

1. $
2. Quotation marks " ".
3. The value of the variable.
4. Assigns a value to a variable (or a formula to a variable).
5. No.
6. B ↑ 3
7. 0
8a. X = +2 * (+3)
  b. N1$ = "ISAAC NEWTON"
  c. LET B4 = 20
  d. K = A * B
  e. ASTRONOMER$ = "KEPLER"

EXERCISES

1.

```
10 REM THIS PROGRAM CALCULATES THE CIRCUMFERENCE
AND AREA OF A CIRCLE
```

```
20  D = 4
30  C = π * D                    (or C = 3.14 * D)
40  A = (D / 2) * (D / 2) * π    (or 40  A = (D / 2) ↑ 2 * π
50  PRINT "THE CIRCUMFERENCE IS"; C    (or simply: 50  PRINT C)
60  PRINT "THE AREA IS"; A              (or simply: 60  PRINT A)
```

2.

```
10  REM SAVINGS ACCOUNT PROGRAM
20  BAL = 933
30  W1 = 45: W2 = 150: W3 = 227
40  D1 = 200: D2 = 100
50  NAME$ = "JOHN DOE"
60  PRINT "SAVINGS ACCOUNT OF "; NAME$
70  PRINT "THE NEW BALANCE IS: $"; BAL − W1 − W2 − W3 + D1 +
D2
```

3.

```
10  REM ASPHALT SEALER PROGRAM
20  L = 35
30  W = 12
40  A = L * W
50  P = 16.99
60  PRINT "THE DRIVEWAY IS"; L; "BY"; W
70  PRINT "THE AREA OF THE DRIVEWAY IS"; A; "SQUARE FEET"
80  PRINT
90  PRINT "ASPHALT SEALER WILL COST $"; P * 3
```

BUILT-IN FUNCTIONS ANSWERS

Questions

1a. 7.45
 b. 5
 c. −8
 d. 7.45
 e. 7
2a. A B S (−5) * SQR(16)   ANS: 20
 b. 3 ↑ 2 * SQR(100)   ANS: 90
 c. 4 * 6 + INT(−6.9)   ANS: 17
 d. ABS(−6) * 2 ↑ 2 * SQR(9)   ANS: 72
 e. 4 * 5 / SQR(100)   ANS: 2

3.

```
10  REM USING THE VAL FUNCTION
20  S$ = "24"
30  PRINT VAL(S$) + 6
```

INPUT ANSWERS

QUESTIONS

1. A is a variable that denotes a number. A$ is a string variable that denotes a string of letters called alphanumerics.
2.

```
10  INPUT "HELLO. MY NAME IS PET. WHAT'S YOURS?"; A$
```

3. You drop out of your program. Either rerun it or type CONT to continue where you left off.

EXERCISES

1.

```
40  LET C = A * B
```

Change the word ADD to MULTIPLY in lines 20 and 10.

2. Line 50 should now read:

```
50  ? "THE ANSWER IS"; C
```

3.

```
10   REM ADDRESS PROGRAM
20   INPUT "WHAT IS YOUR NAME?"; A$
30   INPUT "WHAT IS YOUR STREET ADDRESS?"; B$
40   INPUT "WHAT IS YOUR CITY AND STATE?"; C$
50   INPUT "WHAT IS YOUR ZIP CODE?"; D
60   PRINT "CLR"
70   PRINT "→ → → → → ↓ ↓ ↓ ↓ ↓"; A$
80   PRINT "→ → → → →"; B$
90   PRINT "→ → → → →"; C$
100  PRINT "→ → → →"; D
```

(Note: Only four cursor right arrows are in line 100 because the PET automatically inserts a space before and after a numeric variable. No spaces are inserted before and after a string variable unless you yourself insert them.)

READ-DATA ANSWERS

QUESTIONS

1. Determines the average of Joe Smith.
2. By commas.
3. By commas.
4. $ follows a variable name.
5. Quotation marks.
6. a. No.
   b. Same as before.
7. Second name becomes N$.
8. "Out of data error" is printed.

EXERCISES

1.

```
10  REM READ-DATA PROGRAM
20  READ N$, A, H$, E$, F$, S$
30  PRINT "MY NAME IS "; N$; " AND I AM"; A; "YEARS OLD."
40  PRINT
50  PRINT "I HAVE "; H$; " HAIR AND "; E$; " EYES."
60  PRINT
70  PRINT "MY FAVORITE FOOD IS "; F$; " AND I WOULD LOVE
TO OWN A "; S$
80  DATA "MARY EASTWOOD", 30, "BROWN", "GREY", "PIZZA",
"MAZDA RX7"
```

2.

```
10  REM STUDENT RECORDS
20  DATA "MATH", "1:20"
30  DATA "JOE BROWN", 80, 90, 73
40  DATA "MARY GREEN", 57, 35, 88
50  DATA "JIM BLUE", 45, 63, 72
60  READ S$, T$
70  PRINT "TEST SCORES FOR "; S$; " AT "; T$
80  PRINT
```

```
90  PRINT "NAME", "TEST SCORES", "AVERAGE"
100 PRINT
110 READ NAME$, S1, S2, S3
120 AV = (S1 + S2 + S3) / 3
130 PRINT NAME$; TAB(11); S1; S2; S3; TAB(33); AV
140 GOTO 110
```

3. Add

```
55  DATA "JOAN YELLOW", 76, 85, 82
```

(Note: If the sum is not evenly divisible by 3, the computer will give you a decimal answer.)

4.

```
10  REM SAVINGS ACCOUNT PROGRAM
20  READ NAME$, NUM$
30  DATA "JOHN DOE", "#32-40089"
40  READ BB, D1, D2, W1, W2
50  DATA 500, 200, 300, 150, 75
60  PRINT NAME$; TAB(29); NUM$
70  PRINT
80  PRINT "BEGINNING BALANCE: $"; BB
90  PRINT
100 PRINT "DEPOSITS"; TAB(29); "WITHDRAWALS"
110 PRINT TAB(2); D1; TAB(32); W1
120 PRINT TAB(2); D2; TAB(32); W2
130 PRINT
140 PRINT "FINAL BALANCE: $"; BB + D1 + D2 − W1 − W2
```

(Note: You may have to experiment with the TAB numbers to get good spacing.)

IF-THEN ANSWERS

QUESTIONS

1. The computer jumps to line 70 of the program.
2. The computer goes onto line 50.

3. The computer proceeds to the next program line.
4. They stop the program, thus keeping it from proceeding onto successive lines.
5. The computer jumps to line 60.
6. The computer goes on to line 40.
7. a. CAB
   b. CAT
   c. MMM
   d. DADDY

8.

> 30 IF W1$ < W2$ THEN PRINT W1$; " COMES ALPHABETICALLY BEFORE "; W2$: GOTO 70

Eliminate lines 50 and 60.

EXERCISES

1.

```
10  REM IF-THEN PROGRAM
20  READ A
30  DATA −2.5, 0, 10, 2.345, −7, 6, +22
40  IF A > 0 THEN PRINT A
50  GOTO 20
```

2.

```
10  REM PRINTING PROGRAM
20  COUNTER = 0
30  PRINT "*";
40  COUNTER = COUNTER + 1
50  IF COUNTER < 80 THEN GOTO 30
60  END
```

(Note the use of the counter in the above program.)

COUNTER AND ADDER ANSWERS

QUESTIONS

1. Because X would be reinitialized each time to zero wiping out the sum.

2.

```
40  X = X + 2
40  X = X + .5
```

3. Line 20 initializes both values to 0.
4.

```
:REM ADD 1 TO X
:REM ADD X TO SUM
:REM ON 10TH ITERATION GOTO LINE 70
:REM GO BACK TO LINE 30 AND DO THE PROCEDURE AGAIN
:REM PRINT THE FINAL SUM
:REM END THE PROGRAM
```

5. Counting by 5s
6.

X	0	5	10	15	20
S	0	5	15	30	50

EXERCISES

1.

```
10  REM COUNTING FROM 10 TO 20
20  X = 10: S = 10
30  PRINT "THE INITIAL VALUE OF X IS"; X
40  PRINT "THE INITIAL VALUE OF S IS"; S
50  X = X + 1
60  S = S + X
70  PRINT "X ="; X, "S ="; S
80  IF X = 20 THEN GOTO 100
90  GOTO 50
100  END
```

2.

```
10  REM COUNTING FROM 5 to 15
20  X = 5
30  X = X + 1
40  IF X = 15 THEN GOTO 60
50  GOTO 30
60  PRINT X
70  END
```

3.

```
10  REM KEEPING CLASS AVERAGES
20  SUM = 0
30  INPUT "HOW MANY STUDENTS?"; N
40  PRINT "AFTER EACH NAME TYPE THE SCORE"
50  FOR I = 1 to N
60  READ NAME$
70  PRINT NAME$;
80  INPUT "              ";X
90  SUM = SUM + X
100  NEXT I
110  AV = SUM / N
120  PRINT: PRINT: PRINT
130  PRINT "THE CLASS AVERAGE IS"; AV
140  DATA "MARY SMITH", "JOE JONES", "JOHN DOE", "SUSAN
SHARP," and so on.
```

4.

```
10  REM GIVING THREE CHANCES USING A COUNTER
20  COUNTER = 0
30  A = 7
40  B = 9
50  C = A * B
60  PRINT A; "*"; B; "=?"
70  INPUT X
80  COUNTER = COUNTER + 1
90  IF X = C THEN PRINT "YOU GOT IT!": END
100  IF COUNTER > = 3 THEN PRINT "THE CORRECT ANSWER IS";
C: END
110  PRINT "TRY AGAIN": GOTO 60
```

AND OR ANSWERS

QUESTIONS

1. X must be 0 and Y must be 0.
2. If X = 0 and Y does not equal 0 or if Y = 0 and X does not equal 0.
3. So multiple statements can be put on one line.
4. Add these lines to the program:

```
100 "DO THIS AGAIN? TYPE Y OR N"
110 INPUT A$
120 IF A$ = "Y" THEN GOTO 30
130 END
```

(Any other answer besides Y will automatically cause the program to proceed to line 130.)

5. If the ordered pair is not within the quadrant nor at the origin.

EXERCISES

1.

```
10 REM SCIENTIFIC GEOGRAPHY AWARD PROGRAM #1
20 READ NAME$, TA, NG
30 IF TA >= 80 AND NG >= 80 THEN PRINT NAME$
40 GOTO 20
50 DATA "JOHN SMITH", 64, 81, "JOE JONES", 82, 79, "MARY
BROWN", 93, 84
60 DATA "ANN BLACK", 75, 90, "ROBERT GREY", 97, 89
```

2.

```
10 REM SCIENTIFIC GEOGRAPHY AWARD PROGRAM #2
20 READ NAME$, S1, S2, S3, NG
30 AV = (S1 + S2 + S3) / 3
40 IF AV >= 80 AND NG >= 80 THEN PRINT NAME$
50 GOTO 20
60 DATA "JENNIFER GRANT", 100, 73, 79, 85
70 DATA "MARY BAKER", 54, 92, 84, 80
80 DATA "JOE KELLY", 63, 67, 83, 79
90 DATA "BILL ADAMS", 78, 79, 89, 81
```

(Note: You will get an out-of-data message at the end of both of these programs.)

FOR-NEXT ANSWERS

QUESTIONS

1a. 1
  b. Ones.
  c. 10
  d. 1 to 10.
  e. 60 GOTO 30
2a. 1 to 10
  b. Print the value of X.
  c. Line 30.
3.

    FOR X = 1 TO 10: PRINT X: NEXT X

4.

    20 FOR Y = 10 to 50 STEP 3

5.

    20 FOR Y = 10 TO 0 STEP −1

6. Change line 20 to read: 20 FOR Y = 10 TO 50 STEP .5

EXERCISES

1.

    10 REM COUNTING FROM 15 TO 25
    20 FOR I = 15 TO 25
    30 NEXT I
    40 PRINT I
    50 END

(Note: This program will print out 26 because from 15 to 25 inclusive is 11 times.)
2.

    10 REM COUNTING BACKWARDS FROM 30 TO 20
    20 FOR I = 30 TO 20 STEP −1
    30 PRINT I

```
40 NEXT I
50 END
```

3.

```
10 REM PRINTING A GRAPHIC ACROSS THE SCREEN
20 FOR GRAPHIC = 1 TO 10
30 PRINT "♥";
40 NEXT GRAPHIC
50 END
```

4.

```
10 REM PRINTING A GRAPHIC DOWN THE SCREEN
20 FOR I=1 TO 10
30 PRINT "♥"
40 NEXT I
50 END
```

5.

```
10 REM THE 10 TIMES TABLE
20 FOR I = 1 TO 12
30 PRINT "10*"; I; "="; 10 * I
40 NEXT I
50 END
```

NESTED LOOP ANSWERS

QUESTIONS

1. Change line 20 and 30 to read:

```
20 FOR W = 1 TO 7
30 FOR L = 1 TO 10
```

EXERCISES

1.

```
10 REM TIMES TABLES
20 FOR I = 1 TO 5
30 FOR J = 1 TO 12
40 PRINT I; "*"; J; "="; I * J
50 NEXT J
```

```
60  NEXT I
79  END
```

FLAGS ANSWERS

QUESTIONS

1. -10000
2. Goes to line 80.
3. A very large negative number.
4. Does exactly as Sample program 11.1, adds the numbers, prints out the sums, prints "YOU ARE NOW OUT OF DATA."

EXERCISES

1.
(Note: The following will work for any size set of data.)

```
10   REM DETERMINING AVERAGES
15   REM INITIALIZE ADDER AND COUNTER TO 0
20   SUM = 0: COUNTER = 0
30   READ X
35   REM FLAG COMPUTER TO STOP READING AND GOTO 80
40   IF X = -3000 GOTO 80
45   REM ADD 1 TO COUNTER EACH TIME DATA ITEM IS READ
50   COUNTER = COUNTER + 1
55   REM ADD EACH NUMBER READ TO PREVIOUS SUM
60   SUM = SUM + X
70   GOTO 30
75   REM DETERMINE AVERAGE AND PRINT IT OUT
80   AV = SUM / COUNTER
90   PRINT "THE AVERAGE IS"; AV
100  DATA ....................................................
     ....................................................
     ..................., -3000
```

TIME DELAY AND FLASHING SCREEN ANSWERS

QUESTIONS

1. There is a delay. Nothing appears on the screen though the microcomputer is actually counting.
2. About 7 seconds.

3. Change line 40 to read:

    40 FOR DELAY = 1 TO 7000

4. Jeremy would be printed 1000 times. The screen would never be cleared; there would be no flashing effect.
5. Add or change these lines:

    5 INPUT "TYPE IN YOUR NAME"; X$
    20 PRINT X$

EXERCISES

1.

```
10 REM TIME DELAY PROGRAM
20 PRINT "CLR"
30 PRINT "↓↓↓↓↓↓↓↓↓↓"; TAB (15); "PETS ARE FUN!"
40 FOR I = 1 TO 1000
50 NEXT I
60 PRINT "CLR"
70 PRINT "↓↓↓↓↓↓↓↓↓↓"; TAB(10); "COMPUTERS ARE
GREAT!"
80 FOR J = 1 TO 1000
90 NEXT J
100 PRINT "CLR"
110 PRINT "↓↓↓↓↓↓↓↓↓↓"; TAB(15); "THE END"
120 FOR K = 1 TO 1000
130 NEXT K
140 PRINT "CLR"
```

ON - GOTO ANSWERS

QUESTIONS

1. Prints line 200 (which is choice 2).
   Prints line 300 (which is choice 3).
2. Line 100 (which is choice 1).
3. Computer proceeds to next program line.
4. Computer proceeds to next program line.
5. Add this line:

    75 IF V > 3 THEN PRINT "TRY AGAIN": GOTO 20

6. Add or change these lines:

```
55  PRINT "4: SOUP"
57  PRINT "5: OMELET"
60  PRINT "CHOOSE BY NUMBER: 1, 2, 3, 4, OR 5"
80  ON V GOTO 100, 200, 300, 400, 500
400  PRINT "TODAY'S SOUP IS VEGETABLE": END
500  PRINT "WESTERN OR MUSHROOM?": END
```

EXERCISES

1.

```
10  REM PICK A MATH PROBLEM
20  A = 10
30  B = 3
40  C = 5
50  PRINT "CHOOSE YOUR TYPE OF MATH PROBLEM"
60  PRINT "1: ADDITION"
70  PRINT "2: SUBTRACTION"
80  PRINT "3: MULTIPLICATION"
90  PRINT "4: DIVISION"
100  PRINT "CHOOSE BY NUMBER, 1, 2, OR 3"
110  INPUT X
120  ON X GOTO 500, 600, 700, 800
130  PRINT "INCORRECT CHOICE": GOTO 50
500  PRINT A;"+"; B; "=?"
510  INPUT S
520  IF S = A + B THEN PRINT "RIGHT!": END
530  PRINT "INCORRECT. TRY AGAIN."
540  GOTO 500
600  PRINT A; "−"; B; "=?"
610  INPUT T
620  IF T = A − B THEN PRINT "RIGHT!": END
630  PRINT "INCORRECT. TRY AGAIN."
640  GOTO 600
700  PRINT A; "*"; B; "=?"
710  INPUT U
720  IF U = A * B THEN PRINT "RIGHT!": END
730  PRINT "INCORRECT. TRY AGAIN."
740  GOTO 700
800  PRINT A; "/"; C; "=?"
810  INPUT W
820  IF W = A / C THEN PRINT "RIGHT!": END
830  PRINT "INCORRECT. TRY AGAIN."
840  GOTO 800
```

(Note: This program has been kept simple for ease of understanding. A useful feature that could be added to this program is to have each math problem generated from random numbers. [See Random Number section.] A counter could be built in so the number of tries at a correct answer are limited. Also, a choice in the number of items per drill could be built into the beginning of the program.)

RANDOM NUMBER ANSWERS

QUESTIONS

1. Decimal.
2. No, probably not.
3. No, probably not.
4. Less than 1.
5. Wholes and decimals, that is, mixed numbers.
6. Have whole numbers in them.
7. Are positive integers.
8. 0 to 4.
9. 0 to 5.
10. Change 6 to 7.
11. 1 to 5.
12. Doesn't include 0.
13. 30 B = INT(6 * RND(1) + 1)
14. 2 to 5.
15.

       a. INT(101 * RND(1))
       b. INT(100 * RND(1) + 1)
       c. INT((100 − 5 + 1) * RND(1) + 5)

(Of course, (100 − 5 + 1) can be calculated as 96 prior to typing it into the computer.)

       d. INT((29 − 21 + 1) * RND(1) + 21)
       e. INT((29 − 20 + 1) * RND(1) + 20)

16. 10
17. In lines 50 and 60, change 13 to 6.
18. User keeps getting the same question on the screen.
19. Add the following lines to the program:

      45 COUNTER = 0
      95 COUNTER = COUNTER + 1

    97 IF COUNTER = 3 AND ANS <> C THEN PRINT "THE CORRECT
    ANSWER IS"; C: GOTO 120

20. Add or change the following lines in the program:

    35 INPUT "HOW MANY ITEMS DO YOU WANT IN THIS DRILL?"; N
    40 FOR I = 1 TO N

21. 1 to 10.
22. 1 to 5.
23.

    GOOD WORK! KEEP IT UP!

24. Put :END at the end of each praise statement.
25. User only gets one problem and if the answer is incorrect, the user keeps getting the
     same problem.

EXERCISES

1.

```
10  REM RANDOM NUMBER AND OPERATION PROGRAM
20  X = INT(10 * RND(1) + 1)
30  Y = INT(10 * RND(1) + 1)
40  O = INT(3 * RND(1) + 1)
50  ON O GOTO 100, 200, 300
100  PRINT X; "+"; Y; "=?"
110  INPUT ANS
120  IF ANS = X + Y THEN PRINT "CORRECT": END
130  GOTO 100
200  PRINT X; "−"; Y; "=?"
210  INPUT ANS
220  IF ANS = X − Y THEN PRINT "CORRECT": END
230  GOTO 200
300  PRINT X; "*"; Y; "=?"
310  INPUT ANS
320  IF ANS = X * Y THEN PRINT "CORRECT": END
330  GOTO 300
```

(Note that in division problems it is possible to get decimal or repeating decimal
answers. If this were the case, it is unlikely that a student could get the exact answer,
with the same number of decimal places, as the computer. Therefore, division has not
been included in this exercise.)

2.

```
10  REM GUESSING GAME PROBLEM
20  PRINT "THIS IS A GUESSING GAME"
30  PRINT "YOU MUST GUESS A NUMBER FROM 1 TO 25"
40  PRINT "WHICH THE COMPUTER HAS RANDOMLY CHOSEN"
50  PRINT "SEE IF YOU CAN GUESS IT IN LESS THAN 5 TRIES"
60  PRINT "GOOD LUCK!"
70  X = INT(25 * RND(1) + 1)
80  INPUT "TYPE IN YOUR GUESS";Y
90  IF Y > X THEN PRINT "YOUR ANSWER IS TOO LARGE. TRY
    AGAIN": GOTO 80
100 IF Y < X THEN PRINT "YOUR ANSWER IS TOO SMALL. TRY
    AGAIN": GOTO 80
110 IF Y = X THEN PRINT "YOU GO IT!"
120 INPUT "WANT TO PLAY AGAIN? TYPE Y OR N"; ANS$
130 IF ANS$ = "Y" OR ANS$ = "YES" THEN GOTO 50
140 END
```

PEEK AND POKE ANSWERS

QUESTIONS

1. Heart appears in upper left-hand corner of screen.
2. Another heart appears next to first.
3. A spade appears next to second heart.
4. 83
5. 65
6. In middle of screen.
7. Column 20, row 12.
8. 20 COL = 1
   30 ROW = 25
9. 83, 90, 65, 88
10. 49, 50, 51, 52, 53, 54, 55, 56, 57, 48, 43, 45, 42, 47, 13

EXERCISES

1. Change lines 20 and 30 to read:

   20 COL = 20
   30 ROW = 25

2.

```
10  REM CORNER GRAPHICS PROGRAM
15  FOR I = 1TO4
20  READ ROW, COL
30  DATA 1, 1, 25, 1, 1, 40, 25, 40
40  P = 32768 + (COL - 1) + (40 * (ROW - 1))
50  POKE P,83
60  NEXT I
70  GOTO 70
```

3.

```
10  REM QUADRANT GRAPHICS PROGRAM
15  PRINT "CLR"
20  FOR COL = 1TO40
30  ROW = 12
35  P = 32768 + (COL - 1) + (40 * (ROW - 1))
40  POKE P,83
50  NEXT COL
60  FOR ROW = 1 TO 25
65  COL = 20
70  P = 32768 + (COL - 1) + (40 * (ROW - 1))
80  POKE P,83
90  NEXT ROW
```

CHALLENGE PROGRAMS

1. There are many ways of attacking this problem. Two are presented here:

```
10  PRINT "CLR"
20  READ ROW, COL, W
22  IF ROW = -99 THEN GOTO 100
25  DATA 1, 1, 40, 3, 3, 38, 7, 7, 36, 19, 7, 36, 22, 3, 38, 25, 1, 40
27  DATA -99, -99, -99
30  P = 32768 + (COL - 1) + (40 * (ROW - 1))
40  POKE P,83
50  COL = COL + 1
60  IF COL > W THEN GOTO 80
70  GOTO 30
80  GOTO 20
100  READ R, C, L
105  IF R = -100 THEN GOTO 190
110  DATA 1, 1, 25, 3, 3, 21, 7, 7, 19, 7, 36, 19, 3, 38, 21, 1, 40, 25
120  DATA -100, -100, -100
```

```
130  P = 32768 + (C − 1) + (40 * (R − 1))
140  POKE P,83
150  R = R+ 1
160  IF R > L THEN GOTO 180
170  GOTO 130
180  GOTO 100
190  GOTO 190
```

Another way to write the program is using FOR-NEXT loops instead of IF statements and READ-DATA statements. The first rectangle is done for you; you may try to write the other two.

```
10   FOR I = 1 TO 40
20   P = 32768 + (COL − 1) + (40 * (ROW − 1))
30   ROW = 1: COL = I
40   P,83
50   NEXT I
60   FOR I = 1 TO 25
70   P = 32768 + (COL − 1) + (40 * (ROW − 1))
80   ROW = I: COL = 40
90   POKE P,83
100  NEXT I
110  FOR N = 40 TO 1 STEP −1
120  P = 32768 + (COL − 1) + (40 * (ROW − 1))
130  ROW = 25: COL = N
140  POKE P,83
150  NEXT N
160  FOR J = 25 TO 1 STEP −1
170  P = 32769 + (COL − 1) + (40 * (ROW − 1))
180  ROW = J: COL = 1
190  POKE P,83
200  NEXT J
210  GOTO 210
```

2.

```
10  REM HAPPY FACE PROGRAM
20  PRINT "CLR"
30  READ ROW, COL, SYM
35  P = 32768 + (COL − 1) + (40 * (ROW − 1))
40  POKE P,SYM
45  GOTO 30
50  DATA 12, 18, 78, 16, 22, 78, 16, 18, 77, 12, 22, 77
60  DATA 13, 17, 103, 13, 23, 84, 14, 17, 103, 14, 23, 84, 15, 17, 103, 15, 23, 84
70  DATA 11, 19, 100, 11, 20, 100, 11, 21, 100, 17, 19, 99, 17, 20, 99, 17, 21, 99
80  DATA 13, 19, 42, 13, 21, 42, 14, 20, 34
90  DATA 15, 19, 74, 15, 20, 67, 15, 21, 75
```

GOSUB ANSWERS

QUESTIONS

1.

GOSUB 500

2.

RETURN

3.

130 END

4. Program jumps to subroutine that praises student.
5. Program goes on to line 70.
6.

75 IF ANS <> A THEN GOTO 40

EXERCISES

1.

```
10  REM FAHRENHEIT-CELSIUS PROGRAM
20  PRINT "ENTER YOUR FAHRENHEIT TEMPERATURE"
30  INPUT F
40  GOSUB 500
50  PRINT F; "CONVERTED TO CELSIUS IS"; C
60  END
500  REM SUBROUTINE TO DO CONVERSION
510  C = F - 32 * (5 / 9)
520  RETURN
```

2.

```
10  REM ADDITION PROBLEMS PROGRAM
20  FOR I = 1 TO 5
25  COUNTER = 0
30  X = INT (26 * (RND(1)): Y = INT(26 * RND(1))
```

```
40  PRINT X; "+"; Y; "=?"
50  INPUT ANS
60  COUNTER = COUNTER + 1
70  GOSUB 110
80  IF ANS = X + Y THEN GOSUB 200
90  IF ANS <> X + Y AND COUNTER < 3 THEN PRINT "SORRY. TRY
AGAIN": GOTO 40
100  NEXT I
105  END
110  REM COUNTER CHECK SUBROUTINE
120  IF COUNTER = 3 AND ANS <> X + Y THEN PRINT "THE COR-
RECT ANSWER IS"; ANS
130  RETURN
200  REM CORRECT ANSWER SUBROUTINE
210  PRINT "YOU GOT IT!"
220  RETURN
```

APPENDIX B

GLOSSARY

ADDRESS   Location in memory where a particular piece of data is located.

ALGORITHM   A step-by-step method for performing a particular task.

ALPHANUMERIC   A set of characters made up of letters, numbers, and symbols.

ANALOG COMPUTER   See COMPUTER.

ARITHMETIC UNIT   That part of the computer where arithmetic and logical operations are performed.

ARRAY   Ordered group of addresses where data are stored; each item in an array can be accessed via its ordered position.

ASCII   An international standard code that assigns numbers, letters, and symbols a unique binary code; acronym stands for American Standard Code for Information Interchange.

ASSEMBLER   A program that takes an assembly language program and translates it into the computer's machine code of 0s and 1s.

ASSEMBLY LANGUAGE   See LANGUAGE.

BASIC   See LANGUAGE.

BAUD   The number of bits transmitted per second from one part of the computer system to another. For example, if a computer has a BAUD RATE of 1200 it will transmit 1200 bits per second.

BINARY   See LANGUAGE.

BIT   The smallest unit of information that can be held in a memory location within a computer, usually represented by 0 or 1. BIT is a contraction of the words BInary digiT.

BUG   An error in a computer program.

BUS   Electrical connector between devices of the computer.

BYTE   A group of 8 bits. This group of digits makes up one ASCII character of information, for example, a single letter of the alphabet.

CATHODE RAY TUBE (CRT)   Television-like tube containing an electron beam that displays information on a phosphorescent surface. The screen of the computer is commonly referred to as the CRT unit.

CENTRAL PROCESSING UNIT (CPU)   The internal part of the computer that controls and performs the execution of instructions for the computer system. In the microcomputer, it is the microprocessor.

CHIP   A small piece of silicon that contains electrical circuitry.

CODE   The program written to solve a problem.

COMMAND   An instruction to the computer that is executed immediately by the computer.

COMPILER   Program that translates higher level language programs like FORTRAN and C-BASIC into binary or machine language. A COMPILER differs from an INTERPRETER in that the computer does not act upon the statements until the whole program has been compiled.

COMPUTER   An electronic device that can be instructed by a set of steps called a program to accept data (numbers or characters) and to act on the data using arithmetic or logic operations to produce a result.

ANALOG COMPUTER   A computer that works with continuously varying data within a specified range. Examples of continuously varying data are voltage, temperature, and the tone and pitch of a person's voice.

DIGITAL COMPUTER   A computer that works with separate pieces of data—discrete data—in the binary form of 0s and 1s. It is more efficient than the analog computer in storing large amounts of data.

GENERAL PURPOSE COMPUTER   A computer that can handle many different kinds of problems, for example, the PET.

MAINFRAME COMPUTER   A computer with a very large memory capacity that can handle large amounts of information very quickly. It usually can do more than one job at a time. It is usually the size of a large room. However, with microcircuitry, the distinction between mainframe and smaller mini- and microcomputers has become blurred.

MINICOMPUTER   A medium-sized computer. This computer has a smaller memory capacity than the mainframe but larger than a microcomputer. Sizewise, it will occupy the space of a large desk.

MICROCOMPUTER   A small desk-top-sized computer, often referred to as a personal computer, containing a microprocessor. It may have less memory size than the mainframe or the minicomputers. It generally is slower than mainframes.

COMPUTER LITERACY   The knowledge of what a computer is capable of and the ability to interact with the computer to get it to perform tasks.

CONTROL UNIT   That part of the computer that directs the operation of the computer; it fetches instructions in the program from the memory, decodes and sequences them, executes these instructions, and controls the flow of information to the arithmetic unit.

CORE   Memory of the computer.

COURSEWARE   A computer program written for the specific purpose of aiding a student in the learning of a course or a subject.

CPU   See CENTRAL PROCESSING UNIT.

CRASH   The malfunction of a computer program. The computer stops running and the user has no control over the keyboard.

CRT UNIT   The TV-like screen of a computer where information is displayed.

CURSOR   A symbol, for example, the flashing square on the PET, that indicates where the next character typed in at the keyboard will appear on the screen.

DATA   The general term used to denote the numbers and characters manipulated by the computer.

DATA BASE   A structured collection of information that the computer can access.

DEBUG   To look for and correct errors—bugs—in a computer program.

DISASSEMBLER   A program that translates machine language code into assembly language code.

DISK   See DISKETTE.

DISKETTE   Also called a disk or floppy disk, is a small removable magnetic disk, similar to a phonograph record, that is used to store computer data for later retrieval. It is coated with the same material that recording tape is made of. Standard sizes include 5 1/4″, 8″, and 3″. The Commodore uses 5 1/4″ disks. You cannot read a disk of one size on another sized machine.

DISK DRIVE   Hardware that can rotate the disk and that contains read/write heads to transfer information to and from the disk and computer.

DISK OPERATING SYSTEM (DOS)   The program that allows the computer to access the disk drive while reading information from the disk and while writing information to the disk.

DOS   See DISK OPERATING SYSTEM.

DOT MATRIX   See PRINTERS.

DOWN   Term meaning not functioning, as in, "The computer is down."

ELECTRONIC SPREADSHEET   Computer program using a grid format that can be used for numerical data analysis and record keeping.

ERASIBLE PROGRAMMABLE READ-ONLY MEMORY   Chips that are programmed like RAM and where the memory is nonvolatile until erased by ultraviolet radiation; then they can be reprogrammed.

EXECUTE   The carrying out of a program's instructions by the computer.

FIRMWARE   Programs that are put on chips, for example, EPROMS, and that are permanent and ready for use on power up of the computer.

FLOPPY DISK   See DISKETTE.

GARBAGE   Useless or meaningless data output from the computer.

GLITCH   Error on a computer tape or disk caused by noise or interference during transmission of data.

HARDCOPY   Output information printed on paper.

HARDWARE   Physical components of the computer such as video monitor, disk drive, and keyboard.

HEXADECIMAL   A base 16 number system used by most computers; sometimes called HEX CODE or just HEX; on the PET, this is used when accessing memory through a SYS number.

INITIALIZE   To establish a beginning value for a variable.

INITIALIZE A DISK   To set up a disk so information can be stored on it.

INPUT   Information that is going into the computer, or a device that accomplishes this, such as a keyboard or a card reader.

INTEGRATED CIRCUIT   Small device that contains combined or integrated circuits; often called a chip.

INTERACTIVE   Type of program in which the user interacts with the computer by typing information during the run of the program; a computer that will give an immediate response to a user's keyboard input.

INTERFACE   Electronic circuitry used to connect the computer to other equipment; also the process of joining together two parts of the computer to work as one unit.

INTERPRETER   Program that converts high level languages such as BASIC to the machine language; differs from a COMPILER in that the computer acts upon each statement as it is compiled.

I/O (Input/output)   Refers to devices that input and output information to and from the computer, for example, the CRT unit, line printer, keyboard.

K   Symbol for 1024, often rounded to 1000; it is generally used to refer to the amount of memory bytes the computer has or can use.

KEYBOARD   Typewriter-like device that is used to enter information into the computer.

LANGUAGE   A set of grammar rules, syntax, and code (numbers and words) that the programmer uses to communicate with the computer.

> **ASSEMBLY LANGUAGE**   A language that uses an alphanumeric code to replace some of the binary code of machine language. It makes programming and debugging easier than machine language but less easy than high level languages like BASIC.

> **BINARY LANGUAGE**   Lowest level of computer languages consisting of 0s and 1s; all data and instructions are ultimately translated into binary.

> **HIGH LEVEL LANGUAGE**   Language written in a syntax very close to English. These languages are generally easier to learn than machine language and assembly language. One of the easiest and most widely used languages is BASIC (Beginner's All Purpose Symbolic Instructional Code). Other high level languages include FORTRAN, COBOL, SNOBOL, PASCAL, and so on.

> **MACHINE LANGUAGE**   Lowest level of computer languages consisting of 0s and 1s; same as Binary.

LINE PRINTER   See PRINTER.

LOAD   To copy a program from a disk, tape, or other input device into the computer so it can be used.

LOOP   A programming technique that allows the computer to perform a particular function for a specific number of times.

MAINFRAME   See COMPUTERS.

MEMORY   An area where computer information can be stored.

> **RAM (Random Access Memory)**   Memory inside the computer that is accessible to the user and that can be readily changed. It can be retrieved at will and is volatile or lost when the computer power is turned off.

> **ROM (Read Only Memory)**   Memory inside the computer that is nonvolatile or held there permanently whether the power is on or off. This memory usually cannot be changed and was put there by the manufacturer. The computer language, for example BASIC, and certain operating systems are held in ROM.

MODEM   Device that allows access to a computer via a telephone line.

MONITOR   A TV-like screen on which information is displayed. See also CRT and CATHODE RAY TUBE.

NIBBLE   Half a byte or 4 bits.

OPERATING SYSTEM   A program that controls the input and output devices and allows a person to use the computer. Because each make of computer has a different operating system they cannot communicate directly.

OUTPUT   Information that comes from the computer, or a device that accomplishes this, such as a line printer.

PERIPHERAL   Electronic equipment attached to the computer, such as tape player, disk drive, printer, and light pen.

PRINTER   A device that allows the user to put information on paper.

    DOT MATRIX PRINTER   Prints characters as a number of dots using wires to press the ribbon against the paper, electrodes to burn chemicals from specially treated paper, or ink jets to spray ink. The more wires, the greater the resolution of the type. Nine wires are average, with seven on the small side and twenty on the large side.

    IMPACT PRINTER   Prints characters using hammer-like devices. A standard typewriter is an impact printer. The characters can also be imprinted on a ball or wheel-like device (Daisy wheel). Impact printers are generally slow but yield high quality print.

PROGRAM   An ordered set of instructions written in a computer language that tells the computer what to do. Anything that the computer does requires a program, including the operating system. Programs that are not permanently in the computer but are put in by the user are referred to as "software."

RUN   Command that tells the computer to execute the program in memory.

SAVE   Command that tells the computer to copy information in memory to a disk or tape.

SOFTWARE   Program that can be run on a computer; see also PROGRAM.

STATEMENT   An instruction that is part of a computer program and is executed when the program is run.

SUBROUTINE   A mini program that is called by the main program to be executed many times.

SYNTAX   The grammar of computer language.

SYNTAX ERROR   An error in the language of the program.

TERMINAL   A device that generally includes a display unit, an input device, and the hardware for attachment to a computer.

USER   A person who is using the computer.

WORD PROCESSOR   A program that allows the user to type in and edit alphanumeric text using the keyboard and the screen before a final copy is printed out.

APPENDIX C

BIBLIOGRAPHY

This bibliography is designed to provide for busy teachers some of the better sources of information on computing in the classroom.

PERIODICALS

Classroom Computer Learning (formerly *Classroom Computer News)*. Subscription Dept., 5615 W. Cermak Rd., Cicero, IL 60650. $19.95.

Articles in this publication cover a broad cross section of microcomputer topics, especially illustrations on how microcomputers are being used elsewhere and how microcomputers fit into the educational curriculum. Teachers may not find the majority of articles of practical interest, outside of a rather small "classroom activities" section that gives ideas for early, middle, and upper grades and the usual hardware/software reviews. An interesting feature is the colorful centerfold poster on real world applications of computers.

Compute! Box 5406, Greensboro, NC 27403. $20.00.

This periodical covers a variety of topics in sections devoted to 6502 microprocessor based microcomputers, which include the PET, Apple, and Atari. Topics include programming tips, socioeconomic effects of the computer and sample programs. It is aimed at both the beginner as well as the more advanced user.

The Computing Teacher. International Council for Computers in Education, University of Oregon, 1787 Agate St., Eugene, OR 97403 $21.50.

This magazine is published 9 times per year and is aimed at the microcomputer teacher at the precollege level. Topics of articles have included the impact of microcomputers on education, computer-assisted instruction, and teacher education about computers. There are many programs that can be used in and outside of the classroom, for example, programs that deal with teacher contract negotiations, programs to create drill programs, and programs for preschoolers.

Creative Computing. P.O. Box 789-M, Morristown, NJ 07960. $24.97

This is a fairly comprehensive magazine. It regularly includes hardware evaluations and comparisons, software profiles, and useful program listings. There are occasionally articles relating to microcomputer education. Though not an education-oriented magazine, it is worthwhile for teachers who want to keep abreast of the state of the art in microcomputers.

Electronic Learning. 902 Sylvan Ave., Englewood Cliffs, NJ 07632. $15.00.

This periodical deals with the status and use of the new computer technology in education covering such topics as the impact of microcomputer technology, effective use of microcomputers in the classroom, and research and product development.

School Courseware Journal. 4919 N. Millbrook, Fresno, CA 93726. $124.95 invoice; $99.95 prepaid.

This is a source of well-written and well-documented programs for educational use. It is oriented to both the teacher and the student. It has two programs per issue, and five per year. Examples include a unit on learning to type and a unit on determining the reading level of books being considered for use in the classroom. Permission to copy the student sheets is granted. Printouts of the program, lists of variables used, and subroutines used are also provided. The programs do not make use of the computer's graphic capability, but the programs are of exceptionally high quality.

BOOKS

One has only to visit a bookstore to see the explosion of information about computers and computer languages. While the following is by no means an exhaustive list, it may serve as a starting point for those interested in further reading.

LEARNING BASIC PROGRAMMING

ALBRECHT, R.L., L. FINKEL, and J.R. BROWN (1978) BASIC: A Self Teaching Guide. New York: John Wiley.

BROWN, J.R. (1982) Instant Freeze-Dried Computer Programming in BASIC. Beaverton, IL: dilithium Press.

Compute! (1982) Compute!'s First Book of PET/CBM. Greensboro, NC: Compute Books.

DUNN, S. and V. MORGAN (1981) The PET Personal Computer for Beginners. Englewood Cliffs, NJ: Prentice-Hall.

DWYER, T. and M. CRITCHFIELD (1982) BASIC and the Personal Computer. Reading, MA: Addison-Wesley.

HIRSCH, S.C. (1980) BASIC Programming Self-Taught. Reston: Reston Publishing.

MULLISH, H. (1983) A Basic Approach to Structured BASIC. New York: John Wiley.

OSBORNE, A. and C.S. DONAHUE (1980) PET/CBM Personal Computer Guide. Berkeley: Osborne/McGraw-Hill.

PECKHAM, H.D. (1979) Hands-On BASIC with a PET. New York: McGraw-Hill.

PRESLEY, B. (1983) A Guide to Programming the Commodore Computers. New York: Lawrenceville Press.

ZAMORA, R., W. SCARVIE, and B. ALBRECHT (1981) PET BASIC: Training Your PET Computer. Reston: Reston Publishing.

PRACTICAL BASIC PROGRAMS

ADAMIS, E. (1983) BASIC Subroutines for Commodore Computers. New York: John Wiley.
LAMOITIER, J. P. (1981) Fifty BASIC Exercises. Berkeley: Sybex.
POOLE, L., M. BORCHERS, and C. DONAHUE (1980) Some Common BASIC Programs PET/CBM Edition. Berkeley: Osborne/McGraw-Hill.
RUGG, T. and P. FELDMAN (1979) 32 BASIC Programs for the PET Computer. Beaverton, IL: dilithium Press.

COMPUTERS IN EDUCATION

COBURN, P., P. KELMAN, N. ROBERTS, T. F. F. SNYDER, D. H. WATT, and C. WEINER (1982) Practical Guide to Computers in Education. Reading, MA: Addison-Wesley.
DOERR, C. (1979) Microcomputers and the 3 R's. Rochelle Park: Hayden Book Company.
University of Illinois (1979) Illinois Series on Educational Application of Computers. University of Illinois.
TAYLOR, R. P. [ed.] (1980) The Computer in the School: Tutor, Tool, Tutee. New York: Teachers' College Press, Columbia University.

APPENDIX D

SCREEN FORMAT SHEET

The screen positions for the PET are shown in Figure D.1. The PET has 40 columns and 25 rows. The upper left-hand corner is controlled by the number 32768; the lower right-hand corner is controlled by the number 33767. The formula for determining the number that goes with a certain row and column is Position = 32768 + (COL – 1) + (40* ROW – 1)).

The C64 also has 40 columns and 25 rows. The upper left-hand corner is controlled by the number 1024; the lower right-hand corner is controlled by the number 2023. The formula for determining the number that goes with a certain row and column is Position = 1024 + (COL – 1) + (40* ROW – 1)).

The Vic 20 has 20 columns and 23 rows. The upper left-hand corner is controlled by the number 7680; the lower right-hand corner is controlled by the number 8185. The formula for determining the number goes with a certain row and column is Position = 7680 + (COL – 1) + (20* ROW – 1)).

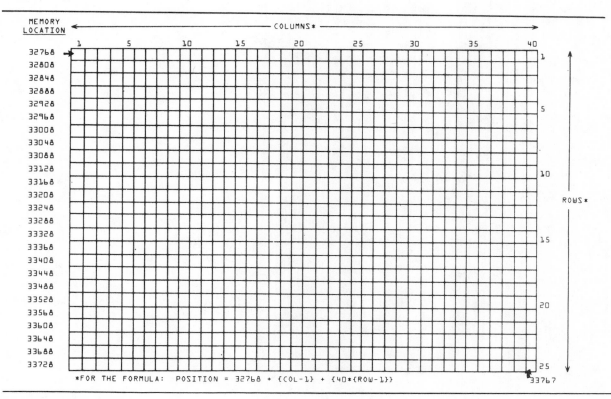

Figure D.1: Screen Format

INDEX

ABOUT THE AUTHORS

Susan Elshaw Thrall received her M.A. (1970) in German from Ohio State University, and a B.A. magna cum laude (1969) in both history and German from the College of Mt. St. Joseph on-the-Ohio. She teaches computer science courses in the Data Processing Program at Santa Fe Community College in Gainesville, Florida. She has taught math and geography at the high school level in Oakville, Ontario, and junior high school in Ohio. Also, she has taught German at Ashland College, Ohio, and Ohio State University. She has continued her education in both mathematics and computer science; she is currently pursuing a Ph.D. at the University of Florida. She programs in BASIC, FORTRAN, and COBOL. She holds Senior Qualifications in educational computer studies and has conducted several workshops on the use of microcomputers in educational curriculum at both Brock University and McMaster University in Ontario. She has also taught computer workshops for the trustees and teachers of Halton Separate School Board in Ontario. Her personal microcomputers include a Lobo Max-80, a TRS-80 Model 1, Commodore 64, and a Timex-Sinclair 1000.

Fred A. Springer received his M.Ed. (1977) in science education from Brock University in St. Catharines, Ontario. He received his B.Sc. (Agr.) in agriculture from the University of Guelph in 1967. He is principal of St. Joseph's School in Acton, Ontario. St. Joseph's is a pilot school for the Holt Electronic Classroom Curriculum Organizor. He has also taught science and math at both the high school level and elementary school level in Ontario. He holds Senior Qualifications in educational computer studies in Ontario. He is a member of the Educational Computing Organization of Ontario. He has been instrumental in developing the microcomputer program in his school system and is a member of the Computer Implementation Team of the Halton Separate School Board. The Halton Separate School microcomputer system is based upon the Commodore 64 and PET microcomputers. His personal computers include an Acorn microcomputer and a Commodore 64.